For Helen Horner,

Hope you enjoy the book

Bob Burdell

People

of the

Pines

PINEY POWER

People

of the

Pines

Text and Photographs by Bob Birdsall
(except as noted)

Design by Jean Sault Birdsall

Contributing Editor, Janet Jackson-Gould

Plexus Publishing, Inc.
Medford, NJ

First Printing, 2007

People of the Pines

Published by Plexus Publishing, Inc.
143 Old Marlton Pike
Medford, NJ 08055

Library of Congress Cataloging-in-Publication Data

Birdsall, Bob.
People of the pines / text and photographs by Bob Birdsall.
p. cm.
Includes bibliographical references.
ISBN 978-0-937548-63-9
1. Pine Barrens (N.J.)--Social life and customs. 2. Pine Barrens (N.J.)--Social life and customs--Pictorial works. 3. Pine Barrens (N.J.)--Biography. 4. Pine Barrens (N.J.)--Biography--Pictorial works. 5. Country life--New Jersey--Pine Barrens. 6. Country life--New Jersey--Pine Barrens--Pictorial works. 7. Community life--New Jersey--Pine Barrens. 8. Community life--New Jersey--Pine Barrens--Pictorial works. I. Title.
F142.P5B57 2007
974.9'48--dc22
2006101504

Printed and bound in Hong Kong.

President and CEO: Thomas H. Hogan, Sr.
Editor-in-Chief and Publisher: John B. Bryans
Managing Editor: Amy M. Reeve
Contributing Editor: Janet Jackson-Gould
VP Graphics and Production: M. Heide Dengler
Designer: Jean Sault Birdsall
Sales Manager: Pat Palatucci
Marketing Coordinator: Rob Colding
Copyeditor: Pat Hadley-Miller

To my wife Jean,
without whose skills, patience, and love
(did I mention patience?)
this book would have never been possible

Contents

FORD

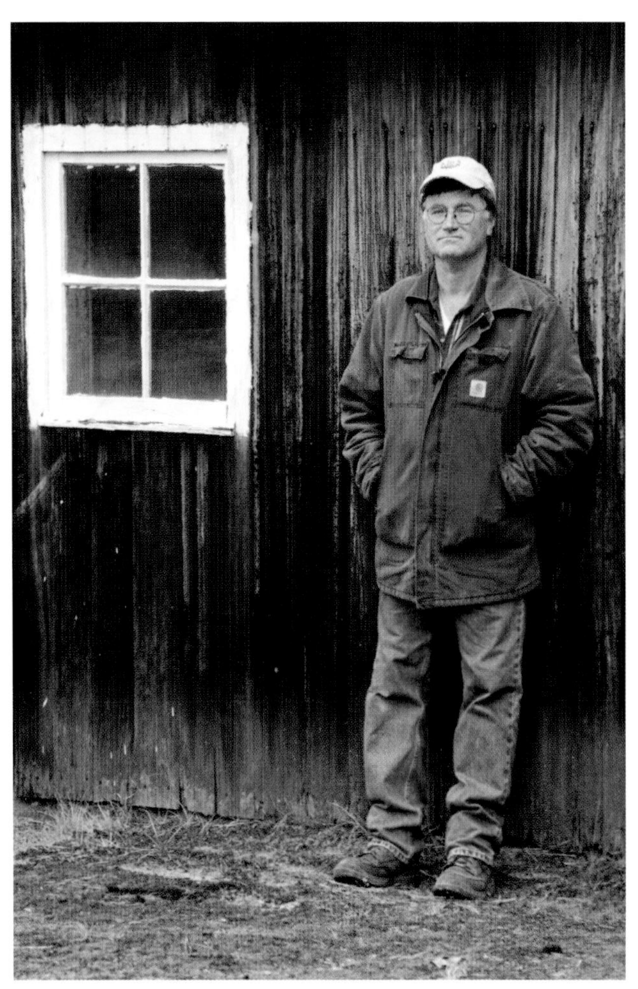

Acknowledgments

I would like to thank the following persons who provided valuable assistance to us in the making of this book:

All the subjects in the book for their enthusiasm and willingness to be photographed and interviewed

Governor Brendan Byrne for his interest and enthusiastic support and for his personal insight into the legislative battle to save the Pinelands

Janet Jackson-Gould for her invaluable writing and editing skills and insight into the Pine Barrens

Ted Gordon, Budd Wilson, and Terry O'Leary for sharing their knowledge of the historical aspects in the book

Special thanks to Ted Gordon for the use of key images from his extensive collection

The staff at Plexus Publishing, Inc. for their outstanding effort and support in making this book happen, particularly John Bryans, Heide Dengler, Amy Reeve, and Shelley Szajner

Elaine and Roy Everett and the Pinelands Cultural Society for their enthusiastic support in making the Albert Music Hall come alive

Carleton Montgomery and Mike Hunninghake of Pinelands Preservation Alliance for their assistance in representing their organization in words and pictures

Doug Brown, brother of Emil Brown and son of Fred Brown, for helping me tell Emil's story

Al Pepper, son of Albertus Pepper, for helping me tell his father's story

Jeff Hirsch for his expert technical support and enthusiastic assistance with the Albert Music Hall group shot

Tom Shuff, a fine young photographer, for his contributions to the J. J. White Cranberry shoot

Patrick M. Brennan for his artistic interpretation of the Jersey Devil

William Heller of the American Legion Post 11 in Mount Holly for his assistance with the Emilio Carranza story

Bill Edwards of the NJ Forest Fire Service for helping me to represent the important role of the Forest Fire Service in the Pinelands

Dan Church and Judy Simons of Simons Berry Farm for allowing me to photograph on their farm

Author's Note: Bill Haines Sr. passed away on February 6, 2007, as the book was going on press. The Pine Barrens lost a great man and I lost a personal friend of more than 40 years.

Introduction

As a young man in the service in 1962, I along with my fellow servicemen read every book that circulated through the barracks. One day I picked up a copy of John Steinbeck's *Travels with Charley: In Search of America*, and the book had an immediate and lasting impact on my life. More than 40 years later as I traveled into the Pine Barrens and began photographing and documenting the stories of the *People of the Pines*, I was constantly reminded of Steinbeck's journey and the parallels to what was quickly becoming an incredible adventure.

Steinbeck and his traveling companion, a French poodle named Charley, set out in a pick-up truck camper to find the "people" of America. Steinbeck shunned the new super highways and instead traveled the back roads; he camped along rivers and farm fields, and in the small villages on his route. These were the places where he hoped to find the American spirit alive and well. Among his numerous encounters in this "Search of America," he interviewed potato farmers in Maine, a fire-and-brimstone minister in Vermont, cowboys in Montana, and bartenders in California.

In his book, Steinbeck relates a conversation with a political reporter with whom he shared a campfire one night. The reporter lamented, "There used to be a thing or a commodity we put great store by. It was called 'the People.' Find out where the People have gone. I don't mean the square-eyed-toothpaste and hair-dye people or the new-car-or-bust people, or the success-and-coronary people. Maybe they never existed, but if there ever were the People, that's the commodity the Declaration was talking about, and Mr. Lincoln."

If Steinbeck were alive today, I would write and tell him, "The People, the ones you've been searching for, they're still here, and they're in the New Jersey Pine Barrens."

The "People of the Pines" share a common bond, and that is their love and respect of the Pines Barrens. It matters not if it's a farmer with a thousand acres or a hunter-gatherer living in a cabin with no running water or electricity—each understands the yearly cycle of the woods and the role he or she plays in it. Each is concerned with protecting the environment, maybe not always from an academic perspective, but certainly from a practical one that comes from generations of living in harmony with the land. These men and women live in a place where a grassroots alliance pushed politics and special interests aside to protect and preserve more than a million acres in the most densely populated state in the U.S.

When I set out to capture the spirit of the "People of the Pines," I was determined to avoid taking "snapshots" or documenting their stories from afar. I wanted, whenever possible, to record them in their environment, performing their vocations and crafts, and to be hands-on in order to truly experience the culture. With this approach, I was able to go clamming with Bob Wilson down at Oyster Creek, accompany Howard Boyd while he checked his beetle traps at the Parker Preserve, join "Snuffy" Fisher on a foxhunt and listen to the "music" of his baying hounds as they chased a gray fox through the woods and cedar swamps, go exploring with Ted Gordon to find a long-forgotten moonshiner's still hidden deep in the woods, and search for the birthplace of the Jersey Devil at Leeds Point with Ken Sooy Sr., a direct descendant of "Mother Leeds." I attended Sunday service in the Jenkins Chapel of the Pines with its own fire-and-brimstone minister, Bob Hagaman, and I joined the Albert Hall musicians for a night of pickin' and jammin' in the "Pickin' Shed." Throughout the entire journey I always knew that at the beginning or end of each day's adventure I could count on a hot cup of coffee and good conversation at Lucille's Country Cooking diner.

It's been said that "the journey is the destination," and this has been one heck of a trip. So thank you, "People of the Pines," for your time, for welcoming me into your homes and lives, and for your willingness to share your stories (and a few tall tales). Most of all, thanks for your friendship. You've shown me why this special place and its precious culture must be preserved at all costs.

Bob Birdsall

Opposite: Bob and Emil Brown, one of the *People of the Pines*

Cranberry and Blueberry Farmer

Bill Haines

"In my opinion Bill Haines is the best farmer and finest gentleman in these woods." —Sammy Moore III

Born in Philadelphia, Bill Haines Sr. spent his summers as a young man working in the family cranberry bogs at Hog Wallow in Washington Township, developing a deep love for the Pines. After attending Rutgers University he went to work full time with his uncle Ethelbert Haines in the family business, commuting daily from Vincentown. Bill took over the operation when his father died in 1965.

Over the next 20 years Bill added many acres to the core farm at Hog Wallow, and today his is the largest cranberry farm in New Jersey. He has made or contributed to numerous improvements in cranberry farming methods. In 1950, Bill helped to establish the Rutgers Cranberry and Blueberry Research and Extension Center in nearby Lake Oswego. In 1965, Bill introduced wet harvesting to the state and increased efficiency and yield per acre to the harvesting process. Despite the remoteness of Hog Wallow, Haines was active in agricultural and community affairs throughout his working life. He was president of the Tru-Blu Cooperative for 25 years and served on the board of Ocean Spray Cranberries from 1945 until 1985.

Cranberry farming is a time-honored enterprise for the Haines family. Bill is the third generation to grow cranberries and his son Bill Jr., a Burlington County Freeholder, is the fourth and well known for his work in farmland restoration. Bill Jr.'s daughter Becky, who is currently active in running day-to-day operations, represents the fifth generation of the Haines family to farm the cranberry bogs at Hog Wallow.

Bill Haines Sr.'s biggest concern for the future of the business involves environmental regulation, but he says it hasn't been too much of a problem to date. "We try to get along with them and they try to get along with us," he declares.

Above: Bill in the mid 1940s

Opposite: Haines Cranberry Bogs

Workers in the packing house in the early 20th century

Photos on this page courtesy of Bill Haines

Ethelbert Haines (front) and cranberry scoopers in the mid-1940s

Harvesting the crop in the mid-1940s

Today, workers in the Haines cranberry bogs use beating machines, which were introduced in NJ by Bill Haines to harvest the cranberries.

Foreman Gerardo Ortiz oversees the operation from atop a truck.

Enrique "Ricky" Zapata, also a foreman, stands knee deep in cranberries in the bog.

Keeper of Legends and Lore

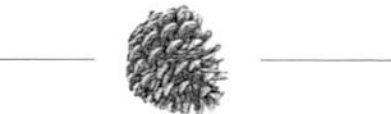

Cliff Oakley

"I always tried to be a good devil..."

Cliff Oakley brought the Jersey Devil and Smokey the Bear alive for more than 18 years to the delight of countless visitors to Pinelands events, only reluctantly giving up the roles in 2005 when he turned seventy-something. Recalling the effect his portrayal had on some children, and even the occasional adult, he says, "I always tried to be a good Devil, but sometimes I may have been too realistic."

Born in Trenton and raised in Ship Bottom, Cliff spent much of his life at the family cranberry farm, Wells Mills Bogs, near Waretown. His grandfather purchased the property in 1936 and built a cabin just in time for the family to celebrate Thanksgiving in the Pines. Wells Mills is now an Ocean County park, but Cliff has lifetime rights to the cabin and still calls it home.

Cliff works at the park as a recreation aid, regaling visitors with lively accounts of the past. Renowned as a Pine Barrens storyteller and historian, he is often tapped by reporters and others seeking to understand the people and places of the Pine Barrens. In addition to the wealth of information stored in his nimble brain, he has accumulated an extensive collection of historical documents dating back to 1760.

The Echo Lake Gunning Club was a group of "all local guys" that Cliff founded in the 1960s. Piney musicians such as the Albert Brothers, Joe and George, would gather at Cliff's cabin on Thursday nights to play and sing while he made spaghetti dinner for them all.

Cliff Oakley is a priceless reservoir of Pine Barrens legend and lore. "If you're going to get involved with Pineys," he says, "you'll find there's no end to history." With Cliff telling the story, you may not mind that at all.

Above: The sign on Cliff's cabin at Wells Mills Park

Opposite: Cliff is the man behind the mask who brings the legend to life.

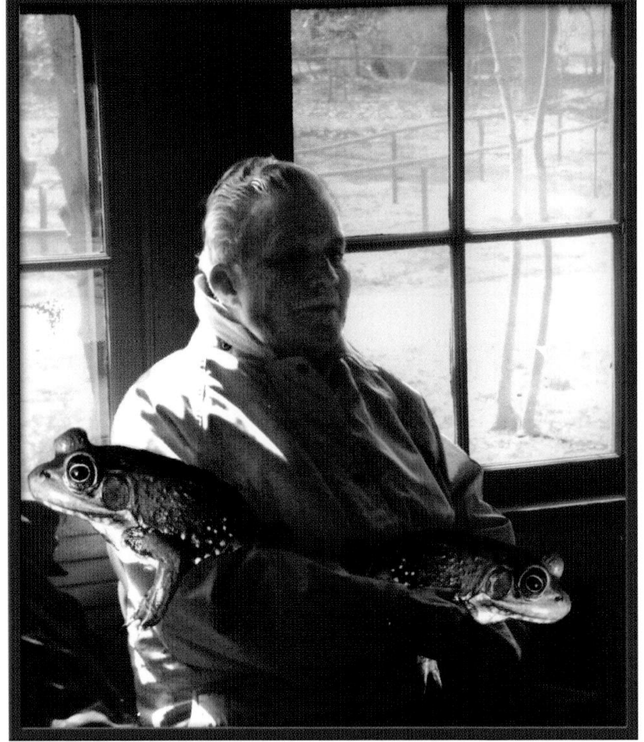

Photo by Walt Bien, PhD

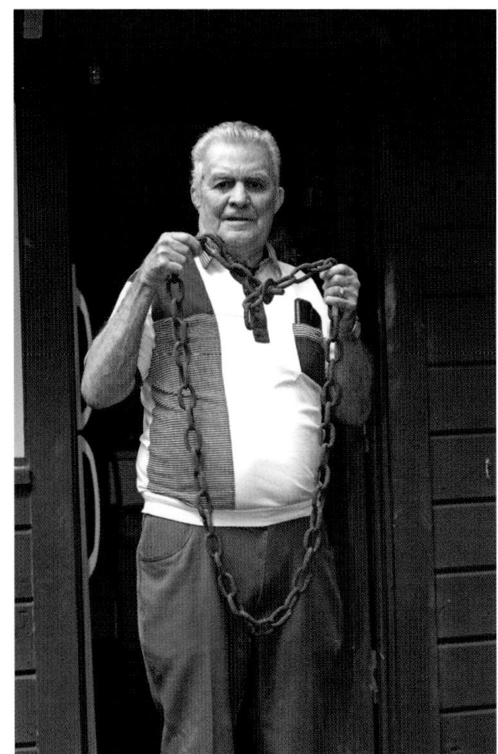

Toby's chain

The Wells Mills Frog Farm

There's a story Cliff saves for folks from outside the Pine Barrens who want to know, "What do Pineys do?" As the story goes, he and three partners once owned a frog farm in Wells Mills, where the average weight of the amphibians was in the 10- to 20-pound range. Asked how the frogs reached such an impressive size, Cliff explains that they thrived on the large local mosquitoes. In fact, he claims that his frogs were so effective at mosquito control that you could camp overnight at the farm without suffering a single bite.

The frog farm became popular in the '60s and was a topic of frequent discussion on a local radio station. One of the frogs—a 27-pound specimen named Toby who was a favorite pet of the partners—grew so big and strong that they had to chain him up. "I still have the chain up in the cabin," swears Cliff. One morning Cliff awoke to discover that Toby had broken the chain and made his getaway. "A lady called the next day from Brookville and said he went over her clothesline," he says. "We never saw him again."

In honor of this beloved story, friends created a framed portrait of Cliff and his legendary frogs (above, left). Look for it on the wall of Lucille's Country Cooking diner.

Cliff's cabin at Wells Mills County Park

Photo courtesy of Cliff Oakley

Children loved Cliff's Smokey the Bear.

Photo courtesy of Cliff Oakley

They approached his formidable devil, however, with cautious curiosity.

JENKINS
CHAPEL
JESUS
SAVES
Visitors Welcome
Worship Service
10:45am
Sunday Scho
Pastor • Bob Hagaman • 609-965-30
James Reid

"Souls were saved here."

Circuit Preacher and Farmer

Pastor Bob Hagaman

Pastor Bob Hagaman beams a welcome as he unlocks the door of tiny Jenkins Chapel, balancing a dish of fresh cucumbers from his garden along with his Bible. He's been the minister of this small nondenominational Pinelands church in Washington Township since 1970 and greets his congregation like the old friends they are.

Pastor Bob came to his ministerial calling on May 2, 1965, when the fire-and-brimstone sermon of a Port Republic preacher brought him to his knees at the altar. In his early days as a man of the cloth he "rode the circuit," preaching at churches in Weekstown, Green Bank, and Lower Bank. When he began at Jenkins Chapel, he conducted services once a month, and later alternated weeks with a friend. Eventually, he took over weekly services at the small green structure that was built as a schoolhouse in 1889.

"My grandfather was a Methodist minister," Pastor Bob recounts. "Before he died he asked my brother and me if one of us would take over for him."

There is more to Bob's life, however, than his work as pastor. He and his wife Pearl operate a 62-acre hay farm, and he is a governor's appointee to the New Jersey Pinelands Commission. A Korean War veteran with a strong desire to serve his nation and community, he was a member of the Mullica Township Committee from 1996 to 2004, serving as deputy mayor for two of those years and as mayor for five. He has served on the township's school board and with the volunteer fire company, and remains a member of the zoning board.

Bob Hagaman says he got involved in public service "because I had the time," and because he thought his faith would be an asset. "I was able to witness," he says.

Opposite: Jenkins Chapel in the Pines, where Bob is the pastor and James Reid is a lay speaker

Pastor Bob and his wife purchased their farm in Weekstown more than 50 years ago. They initially had dairy and beef cows, but now farm only hay.

The barn, built in 1924, is still in use.

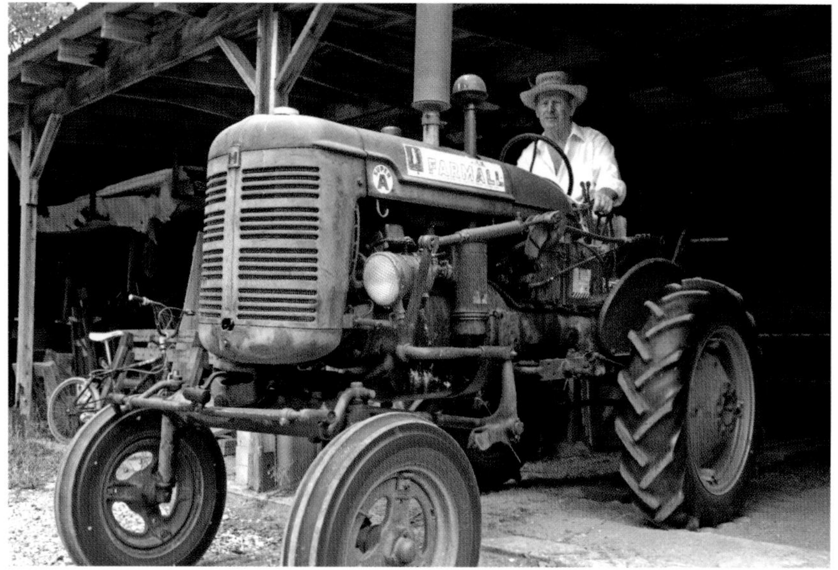

Pastor Bob still uses his 1952 Farmall tractor for the harvest.

Photo by Ted Gordon

Jenkins Chapel in the Pines

Jenkins Chapel in the Pines began as a schoolhouse for local children in 1889. In the early 20th century it was purchased by the Episcopal Church and used by circuit preachers for many years, but by 1970, when this photo was taken, it was no longer in use. In the spring of that year, Pastor Bob began preaching services at the little chapel. In 1978 the pastor and his sister Harriet formed a small corporation and purchased the building from the Episcopal Diocese for $2,000 and established it as a nondenominational chapel.

"Don't let technology get in the way of the dirt."

Charles I. (Budd) Wilson Jr. lives in a house in Green Bank that dates back at least to the 1850s and perhaps to the 1820s—a suitable abode for a passionate archaeologist and historian. His unsurpassed knowledge of the Mullica River Basin has its roots in the summers he spent with his parents in a cottage on the banks of the river.

Budd was a pioneer in the field academics now call "Historical Archaeology," combining a degree in history with a love of archaeology. For more than 20 years he worked in the Pine Barrens, leading major digs at Allaire, Atsion, Harrisville, and Martha's Furnace. At Batsto, he helped excavate the ore boat and iron furnace, worked as a carpenter, and later excavated the site's vanished glass works. Over the span of a 40-year career, he has participated in archaeological projects throughout New Jersey, but his heart has always been in the Pines.

"This was Pittsburgh, not paradise," Budd says, referring to the Pine Barrens in the days of the iron forges and furnaces. At the peak of the iron industry in the early 19th century, Budd says there were 13 furnaces operating, consuming nearly 20,000 acres of forest for charcoal annually and cutting over each acre about every 25 years.

"I get upset sometimes that no one is restoring historical sites and that no primary research is being done," Budd laments. He is encouraged, however, that the mansion at Atsion is slated for restoration. The project will utilize data he unearthed more than 20 years ago.

Now retired, Budd Wilson is not resting on his laurels, nor is he sitting still. His advice to young archaeologists? "Don't let technology get in the way of the dirt."

Above: Budd Wilson's home on the Mullica River

Opposite: Budd surveys the area around the sawmill at Batsto.

Historical Archaeologist

Budd Wilson

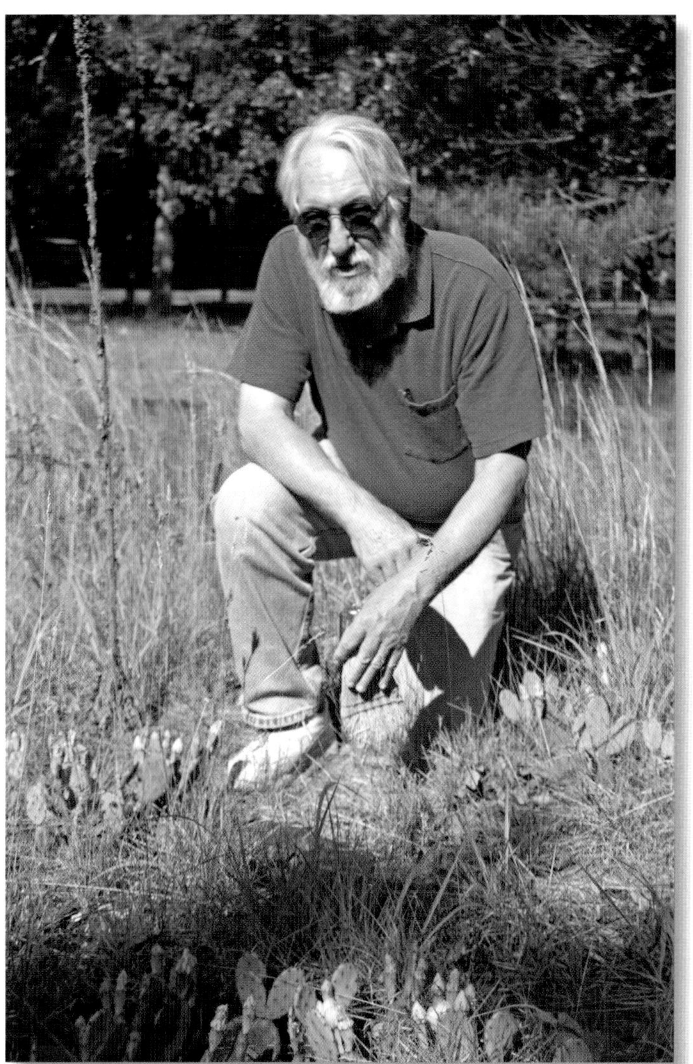

Photo by Ted Gordon

The Martha Furnace excavation site

Photo courtesy of Budd Wilson

A young Budd at the Martha furnace excavation

Martha Furnace Excavation

In July 1968, Budd Wilson and a small group of fellow archaeologists began the "dig" at Martha Furnace—one of the most important area furnaces during the height of the iron industry in the Pine Barrens. Located deep in the woods south of Speedwell on the Oswego River, Martha Furnace was built in 1793 by Isaac Potts, who named it in honor of his wife. As the iron industry went into decline in the Pines in the 1840s, Martha Furnace survived for many years because of its isolation and importance to the local community, but time and nature finally took their toll.

Budd and his team worked tirelessly throughout the summer and fall of 1968, using trowels and whisk brooms to gently expose the remains of the furnace. After the excavation and study were complete, their findings were meticulously documented. The fragile furnace was then reburied to protect it from further deterioration and "potholers"—amateurs who dig only to carry away artifacts.

The rediscovery of Martha Furnace provided the opportunity to excavate the only Pine Barrens iron furnace with above ground remains. It is important also because of the rich historical data that exists to complement the archaeological documentation, the "Martha diaries." These diaries, kept by a furnace employee, document the day-to-day workings of the furnace and life in the surrounding community through the years 1808–1815. Today, along with the Batsto Iron Furnace, Martha Furnace remains one of only two iron furnaces in the Pine Barrens to be excavated. Budd Wilson was on the job for both of these historic excavations.

Opposite: Batsto Mansion in the spring

Piney Hunter-Gatherer

Bill Wasiowich

"I'm happiest in the woods. Just me with nobody else around."

Bill Wasiowich is a "Piney" and proud of it. He is one of the last hunter–gatherers to make a living from the land, following the seasonal cycle that sustained generations before him. In the spring and summer he harvests sphagnum moss and in the winter he hunts or picks "pineballs"—pinecones used in the floral industry. He cuts blueberry stalks, or hogbrush, which is used by craft makers, and splits and stacks firewood for sale and to heat his home.

Bill lives in a hunting cabin built around 1910 that he rents from a gun club for $1,000 a year. Tucked into the pine woods of eastern Burlington County, it has electricity and running water, but the restroom is an outhouse. He has no boss and his time is his own, giving him a freedom seldom experienced in today's world.

Independent and resourceful, Bill builds most of his own equipment, including the sphagnum moss press and the conveyer belt he uses for sorting blueberries. He was featured in John McPhee's 1968 book, *The Pine Barrens,* and is well aware of his status as the last of the Piney hunter–gatherers. Instinctively wary of first-time visitors, he will proudly share stories of his life in the woods and of days past with those who have earned his trust.

It's getting harder and harder for Bill Wasiowich to sustain his lifestyle. As the state buys up land for preservation, there is more regulation and fewer places to gather. Still, he perseveres, pursuing a way of life that will soon be relegated to Pinelands legend and lore.

Opposite: Bill at his home in the Pines

The shed serves as the workroom where many of Bill's tools are made.

Bill at his workbench in the shed

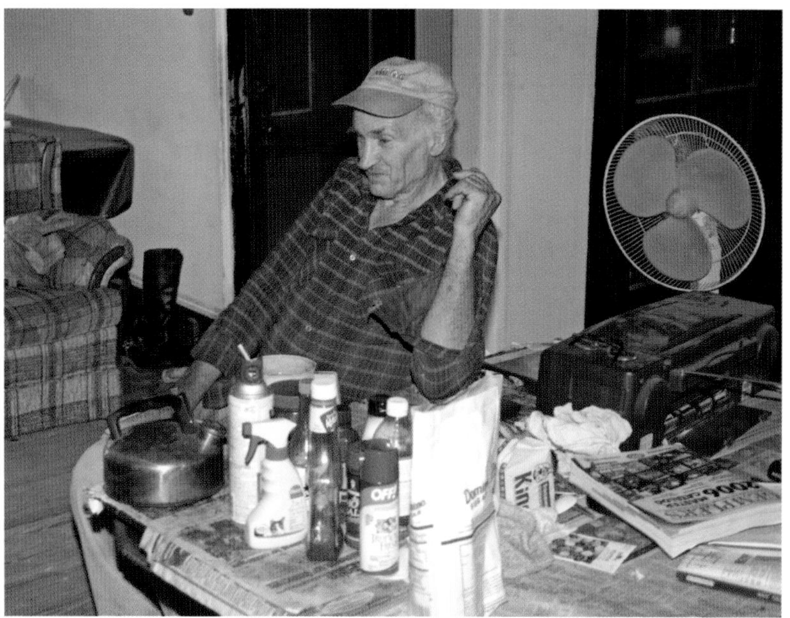

Inside the hunting cabin Bill calls home

Bill presses his gathered moss in his homemade press.

Photo by Ted Gordon

The moss is then air-dried in his yard.

Bales of moss stand ready for market in the shed.

Bill loads hogbrush, stalks from blueberry bushes, onto the truck for market.

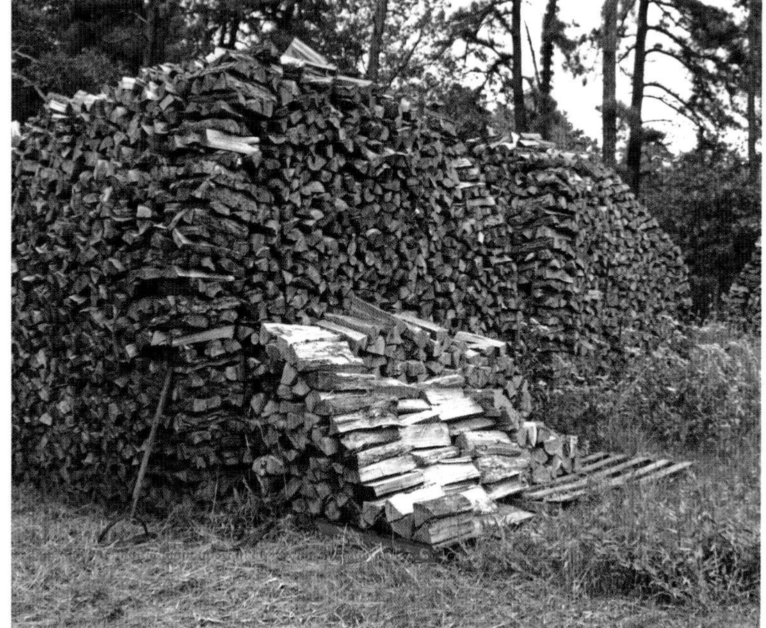

Bill cuts and neatly stacks his wood by hand.

LUCILLE'S
COUNTRY COOKING
1496
LUCILLE'S
Coca-Cola
LUCILLE'S
COUNTRY
COOKING

Business Owner and Volunteer

Lucille Bates

"It doesn't seem to matter where they're going to or where they're coming from, we're halfway."

Lucille Bates is the proprietor of Lucille's Country Cooking, a Warren Grove eatery that is legendary for its down-home cooking. Although it's located on a remote stretch of Route 539, people still stop. Lucille says that's because it's halfway to wherever they are going. "It doesn't seem to matter where they're going to or where they're coming from, we're halfway," she says. Asked what makes her remote Pine Barrens restaurant so successful, Lucille observes that "hospitality and chit-chat are free and the coffee ain't bad either."

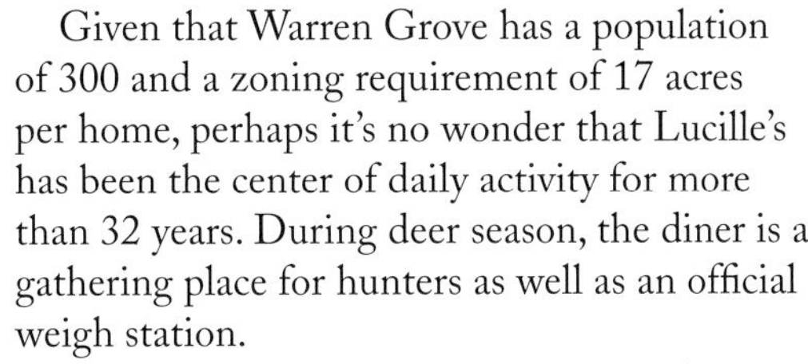

Given that Warren Grove has a population of 300 and a zoning requirement of 17 acres per home, perhaps it's no wonder that Lucille's has been the center of daily activity for more than 32 years. During deer season, the diner is a gathering place for hunters as well as an official weigh station.

Lucille Bates is more than a short-order cook—she's a lynchpin of her community. She has been honored for her work on behalf of abused women and children, both as a member of domestic violence and sexual assault response teams and as a court-appointed advocate for foster children. She regularly helps her customers, many of them senior citizens, by providing transportation, and has welcomed them into her home for bountiful holiday dinners. Lucille has been a Girl Scout leader, an officer of the local PTA, the first female secretary of the Stafford Township Lions Club, and vice president of The Business & Professional Women of Southern Ocean County (BPW SOC). She remains active with the Stafford Historical Society.

"I love volunteering to make a difference," Lucille says. "Even if it's only one person that I can help."

Opposite: Lucille's Country Cooking diner on Route 539 in Warren Grove

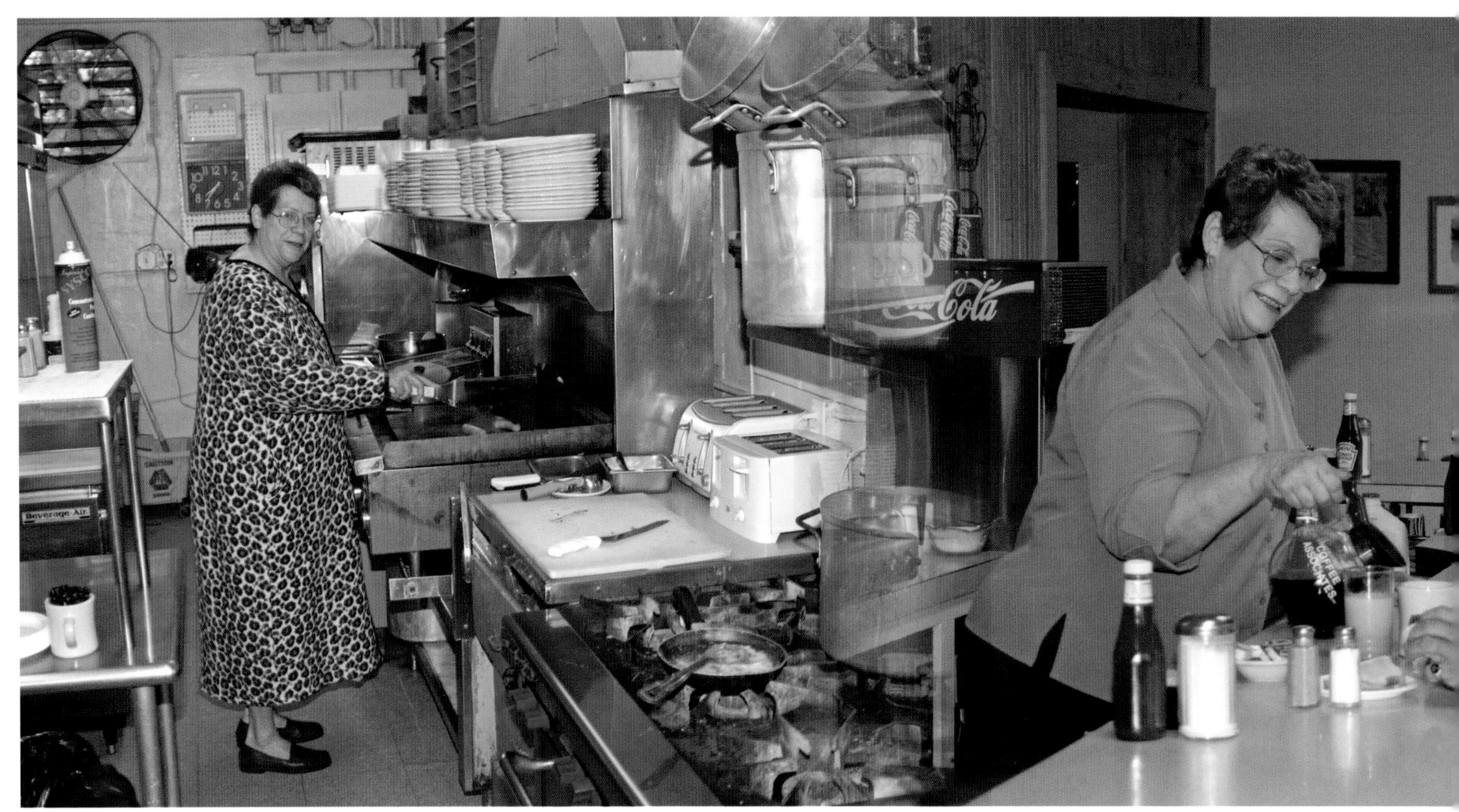

"Only my customers who come in before 8 A.M. see me like this!"

All in a day's work: Beginning at dawn in her bathrobe til the diner closes at 3 P.M., Lucille serves up "down home" food and hospitality.

EARLIN'S HUNTING CLUB

Deer Hunter

Johnny Earlin

"Pop Pop, come quick! I think I got one!" —Johnny Earlin Jr., at age 11, after shooting his first deer

Nowhere are the rites of passage more evident than in the gunning clubs of the Pine Barrens, some of which trace their origins well back to the 1800s. The Earlin Gun Club was founded in 1955, when Johnny Earlin's grandfather and a group of 40 of his friends purchased 35 acres deep within Greenwood State Forest. They built a cabin for use by club members during deer season, complete with a pot-bellied stove and bunk beds. Johnny is the third-generation to hunt with the club, following in the footsteps of his dad Walt. Johnny's son Johnny Jr., at 14 years old, is the fourth-generation Earlin to belong to the club; he shot his first deer at age 11.

As a young boy, Johnny remembers hunting with his grandmother and his aunt, both of whom enjoyed staying at the cabin. Johnny claims they could brave the cold and track a wounded deer as well as anyone in the woods. His grandfather, a legendary deer- and foxhunter in the Pine Barrens, owned Earlin Chevrolet in Browns Mills, and during deer season, the members would proudly hang their deer out in front of the Chevrolet showroom. Johnny, his father Walt, and his son Johnny Jr. continue to enjoy the camaraderie provided by the club. After a day's hunt, they gather at the cabin to play cards, swap tall tales around a fire, and follow the tradition of instilling a love of hunting and respect for the land to the next generation.

Above: The sign at the Earlin Gun Club

Opposite: Smoke rises from the gun club cabin as opening day draws near.

The bunkhouse at the back of the hunting club cabin

A winning hand before opening day is a good sign.

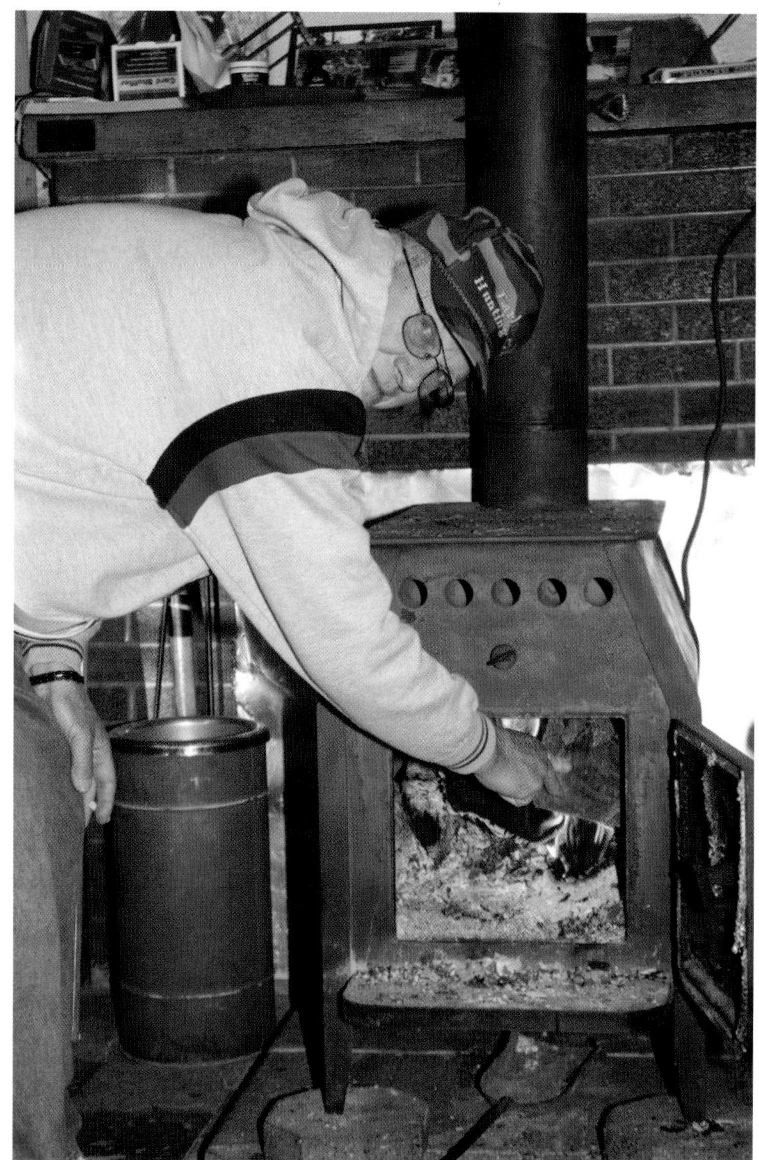

Walt Earlin puts wood on the fire in the cabin's woodstove.

Johnny Earlin Jr. splitting wood for the upcoming season

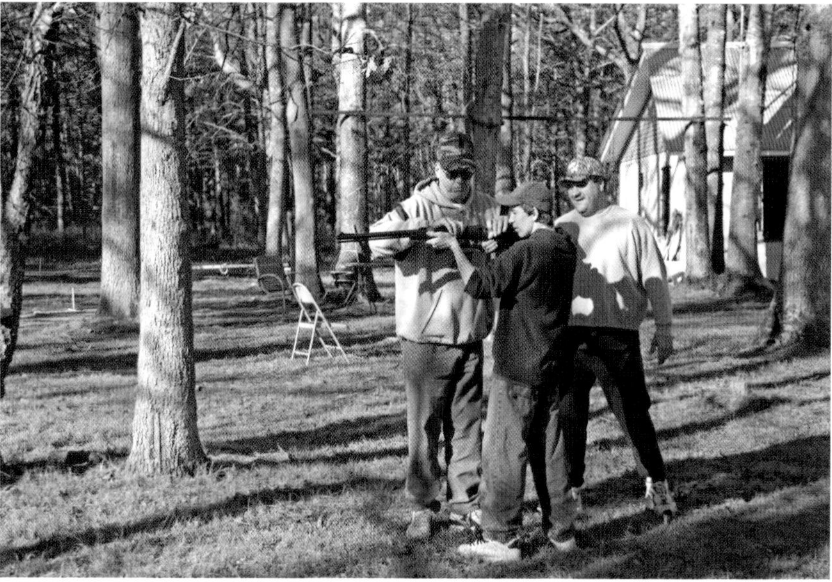

Johnny Jr. gets safety pointers from Grandpop Walt.

Johnny Jr. fires his muzzle loader while Dad and Grandpop look on.

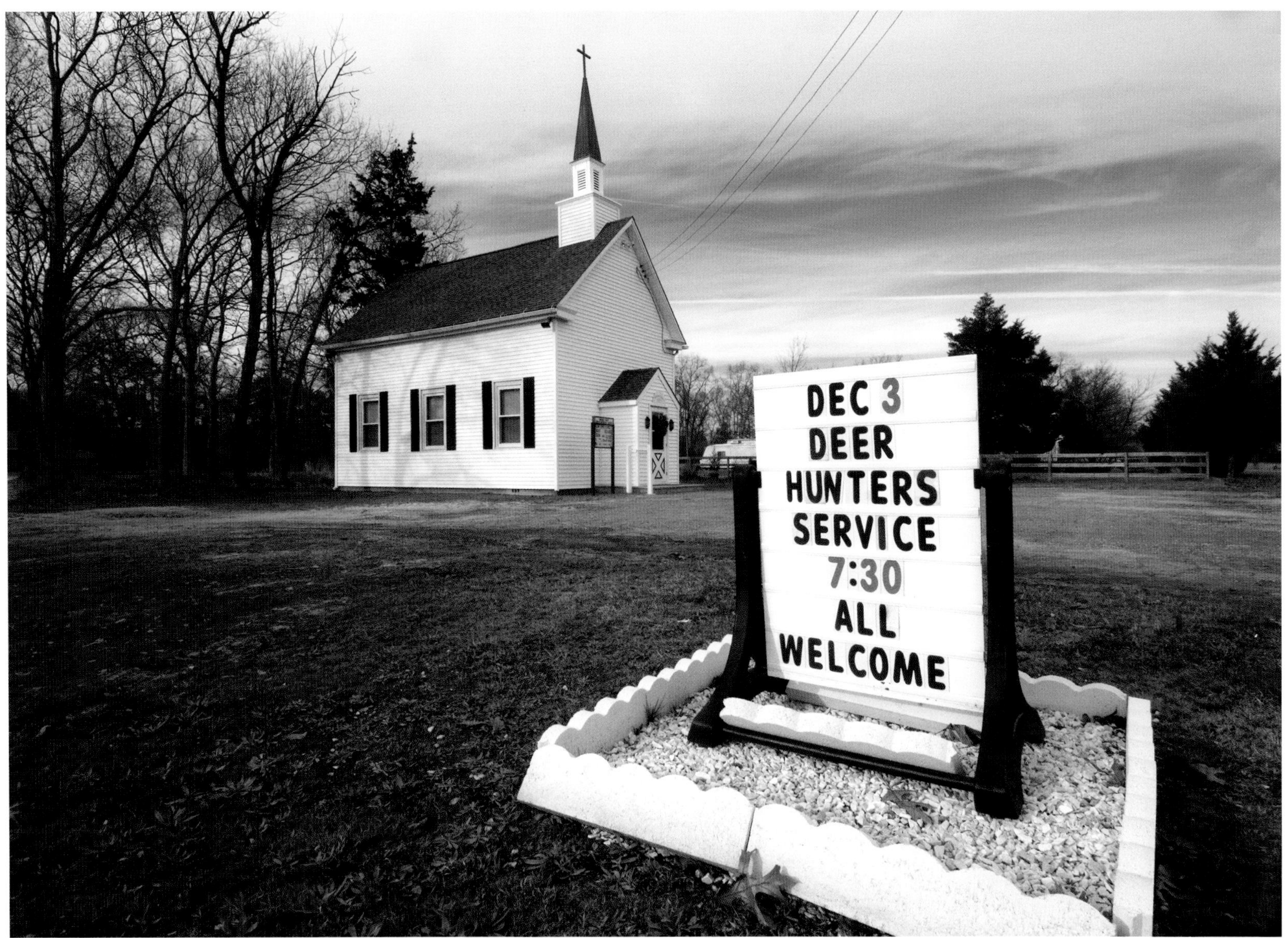

Ever since the mid-1960s, on the night before shotgun hunting season opens, a service is held at the United Methodist Church in Warren Grove. According to Reverend Barry H. Steinmetz, the pastor at the church for the past six years, the service is attended by hunters from many area gun clubs. Together in the small church, with the anticipation of the new season just hours away, they pray for the safety of all hunters in the woods. Their simple prayer is recorded in the service bulletin for all to recite: "Dear God, Jesus, and the Holy Spirit, please protect these hunters while they are in the woods hunting. Amen."

Reverend Barry H. Steinmetz conducts the service.

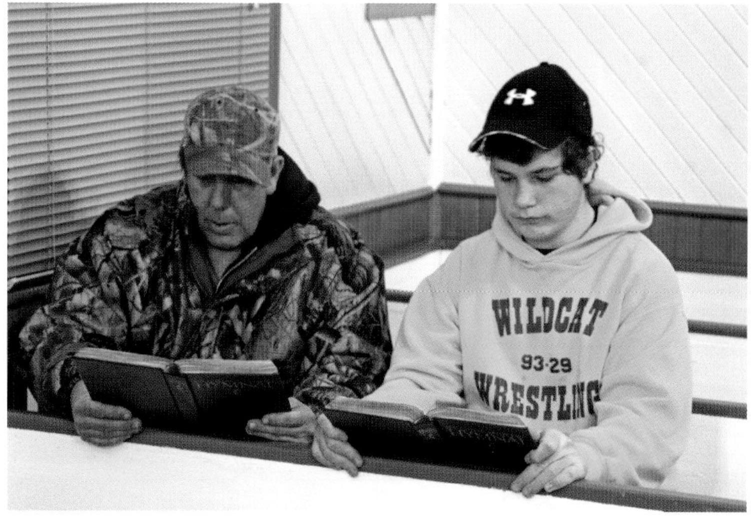

Sheridan Durand and his son Nicholas on the eve of Nicholas's first hunting season

Reverend Steinmetz, a lifelong Piney who was raised on a chicken farm in Tuckerton, plays guitar during the hymns.

Ted Brewer tracks a wounded deer on opening day.

Decoy Carver and Storyteller

Gary Giberson

"By far the greatest gifts my grandfather gave me were telling stories and carving decoys."

In 1637, the Giberson family settled in Chestnut Neck, one of the first settlements on the Jersey coast, and was split between Tory and Patriot sympathies during the War of Independence. After the war, the Tory branch of the Gibersons migrated to Nova Scotia, Canada, while the Patriot side of the family remained on the Mullica River. It is from this branch that Gary Giberson traces his ancestry.

As a boy, Gary learned the craft of decoy carving from his grandfather Alonzo Giberson. Gary makes his decoys from Atlantic White Cedar harvested from his own property, a use that is grandfathered now that cedar swamps are a protected habitat. Wood, of course, is the key ingredient in decoy making, and Gary knows his material: He claims he can tell white cedar taken from the north side of the Mullica from that cut on the south.

Gary is an avid duck hunter, trainer of retrievers, and photographer. Although it is illegal to use corn to lure ducks, he strives to make his decoys look like they are engaged in a grain "feeding frenzy." The distinctive high heads, arched necks, and downward-pointing bills make his carvings stand out. Gary boasts that ducks don't circle his decoy rig, but make a beeline into the heart of it.

"Gary's Garage" is a replica of a 1930s gas station, built and lovingly maintained by Gary in Port Republic, where he has been mayor for over 20 years. He and his wife Niki also run Swan Bay Folk Art Center where they teach basketry, doll making, and other traditional crafts. The Gibersons observe the time-honored traditions of American craftsmen and women, and take great pleasure in sharing their skills and stories at historic sites and festivals throughout the area.

Above: The Gibersons' sign

Opposite: A mallard decoy carved by Gary

Photo by: Niki Giberson

Gary plays the part in his 1931 Model A Ford roadster.

Opposite: Gary's replica of a 1930s garage and his "Piney hillbilly" truck can be found in his backyard. His road kill take-out bucket adds to the "flavor."

GARY S
GARAGE
Mobilgas
PRODUCT OF A SOCONY-VACUUM COMPANY
Mobilgas
STOP YOUR MOTOR
NO SMOKING
Please
GARAGE Firestone TIRES GASOLINE
GAS 13 8/10
TAX 4¢
TOTAL 17 8/10
Mobiloil
30¢ 35¢
ICE COLD
NEHI
GAS
17¢
TODAY
DRINK
NEHI
Sold Here
Ford
GARGOYLE
Mobiloil
VACUUM OIL COMPANY
Mobilgas
Exide
BATTERIES
WHITE EAGLE GASOLINE
Mobiloil
Ask for-
GARGOYLE
Mobiloil
Authorized Service
VACUUM OIL COMPANY
"TAKE OUT"

Folk Artist

Niki Giberson

"We're one generation away from losing these arts."

Animals were Niki Giberson's passion while she was attending Stockton State College, pursuing a degree in animal behavior. But life was to hold some surprises. During a school break, she asked the resident spinner at Batsto to teach her to spin and weave. "Come for one class," the spinner said. "If I like you, you can come back." That was the beginning of a yearlong apprenticeship, and it soon became clear that Niki's true calling was in the folk arts. She returned to college with new goals and received a degree in Early American Crafts and Culture, a curriculum encompassing business, history, and art.

Niki keeps the historic arts alive at Swan Bay Folk Art Center, which she and her husband Gary built together on 55 acres of land in Port Republic. There she teaches spinning, basket weaving, and doll-making. She raises her own sheep and uses their wool for spinning and creating woolen goods, a true "sheep-to-shawl" enterprise.

In Niki's popular basket-making classes, she often teaches several patterns at a time. Gary supplies some of the handles for the baskets, carving them from white oak gathered in the Pine Barrens. Some of her basket handles are shed deer antlers "carved by God," she says with a smile. Many of her baskets are sold at local stores, including historic Buzby's General Store in Chatsworth.

"When people come to my studio they create their own piece of history," Niki says. She is eager to keep these historic folk arts alive in her own family and has taught each of her three daughters these skills so that they, too, can carry on the old traditions.

Above: One of Niki's baskets

Opposite: Niki spins wool on a traditional spinning wheel.

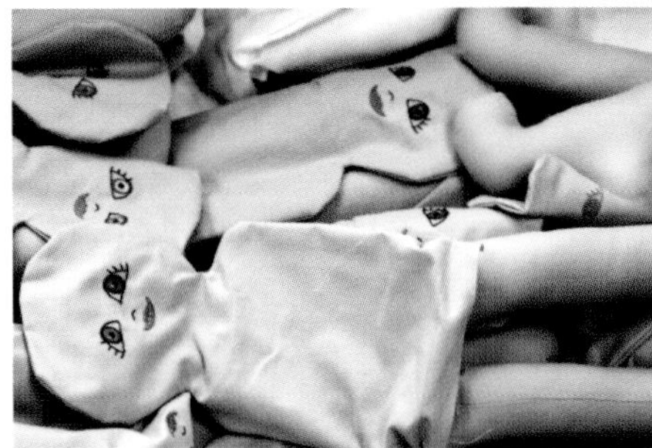

Dolls and animals wait to be chosen by a child in one of Niki's "Create a Friend" workshops.

Niki helps the children stuff and sew their new friends in her studio.

Each friend gets a name chosen by the child and a birth certificate signed by Niki.

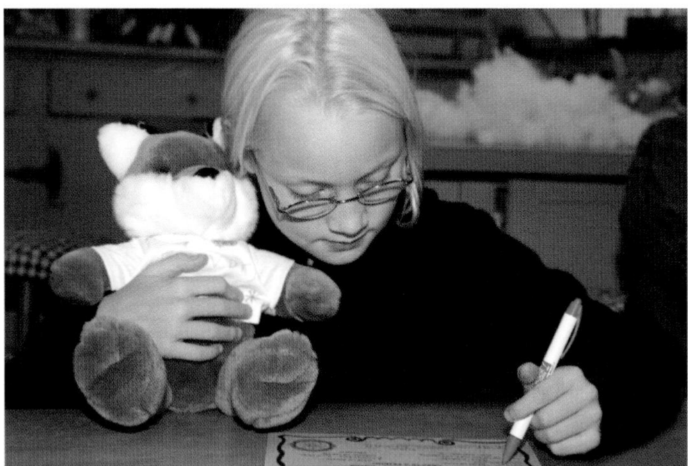

"Trevor" the clever fox gets his birth certificate.

Opposite: Niki's Friday night "Friendship" basket-making class in action

State Park Ranger

Lt. Greg Langan

"My job is to protect the forest for future generations. That's why I do what I do."

Lieutenant Greg Langan patrols miles of sand trails in the state forests within the Pinelands, assisting visitors, routing troublemakers, and safeguarding the environment. He considers the greatest threat to this fragile ecosystem to be the misuse of off-road vehicles, which are illegal in the state park system. "The cumulative effect on bogs and ponds is devastating," he says.

Greg leads the troop of 25 Parks and Forests police officers that protect the department's southern region, a relatively small force considering the enormous acreage of Wharton, Bass River, Belleplain, Parvin, and Brendan Byrne State Forests, plus Cape May Point and Corson's Inlet State Parks.

He's been part of the action for 29 years, so the extent of human folly holds few surprises for him. With the advent of SUVs and cell phones (which often don't work in the Pine Barrens) more people are venturing more deeply into remote areas, often getting lost or stuck in deep sand. Their activities increase the pressure on sensitive natural resources and habitats.

In addition to rescuing those who venture off the beaten track, Greg's duties include patrolling campgrounds, investigating hunting violations, posting boundary markers, removing snakes from areas of human contact, and working with local communities on a range of projects. He produces educational programs, organizes fishing tournaments, and helps newcomers appreciate and learn to feel at home in the woods.

Greg feels the increasing black bear population in the Pinelands should not present a problem for recreational users (he notes that blueberry farmers take a different view). "There is enough natural food in Wharton and Brendan Byrne State Forests to keep the bears out of the camping areas."

Gary Langan's favorite part of his work is the opportunity to protect natural resources. "I consider myself a frontline environmentalist," he says. "I'm there to protect the forest for future generations."

Above: A black bear

Opposite: Greg's favorite spot, the Skit Branch of the Batsto River

Lt. Langan in Wharton State Forest

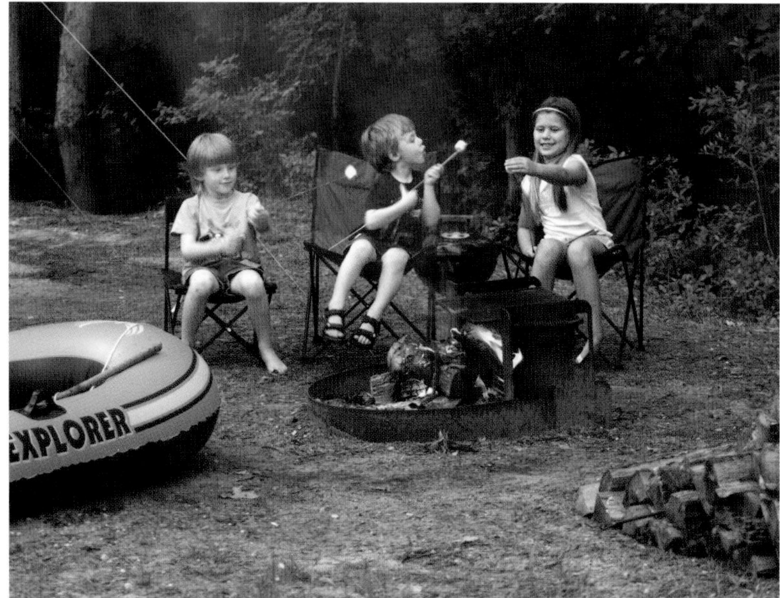

Family camping and swimming are popular activities in the state parks and forests that Greg protects.

Kayaking on the Oswego River

Opposite: A campsite in Wharton State Forest

Colema

Environmental Educator and Mentor

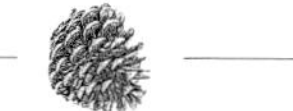

V. Eugene Vivian, PhD

"Eugene Vivian planted many acorns that grew into mighty oaks." —Dr. Robert Elder

Dr. V. Eugene Vivian's name is synonymous with environmental education in the Pine Barrens. As science department chair at Glassboro State College (now Rowan University), "Doc" secured grant funding and formed the Conservation and Environmental Studies Center (CESC) at Whitesbog. There he assembled a staff of students and advisors who rank among today's leaders in environmental education.

The CESC focused on Pinelands plant communities and animals, and was led by Doc from 1968 until 1984 with the following objective: "We wanted people to come here and exchange information and learn from each other." Another goal was to model environmental education for teachers who came for field trips, empowering them to teach about the environment back at school. By 1969 more than 40 school districts were involved in the program and Doc Vivian received the National Conservation Educator of the Year Award.

Doc Vivian grew up in Paterson, NJ and received his PhD at New York University. As a Boy Scout he was awarded an "Acorn" emblem for his ability to name 500 species of plants. With the emblem came additional duties that included training others. Having reached that level, one of the things he is most grateful for was the opportunity to teach.

After resigning from the CESC in 1981, Doc formed his own consulting firm. He and his associates, including Terry O'Leary, helped establish wetland boundaries and documented evidence of endangered plants and wildlife. Although his accomplishments are many, environmental education is where Dr. Eugene Vivian has left his mark.

Above: Eastern fence lizard

Opposite: Doc and John Szczepanski, a former student, on an environmental study at Whitesbog in 1987 (Photo by Al Zacharka)

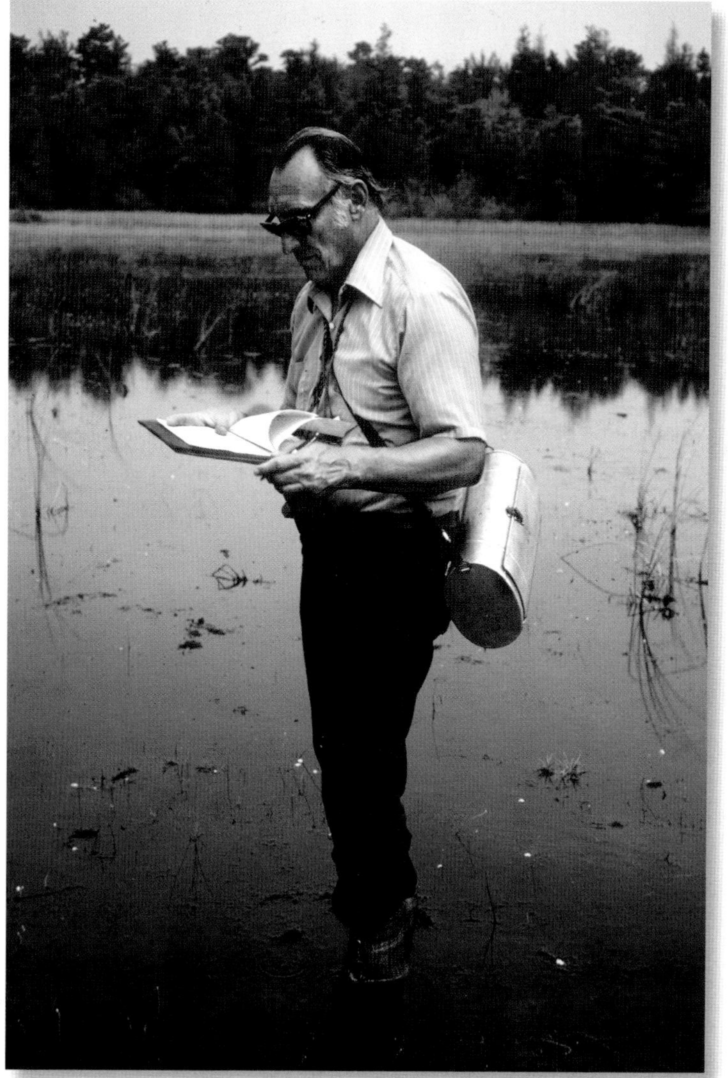

Photo by Ted Gordon, 1979

EXIT
TREES DO MORE THAN
JUST STAND THERE
GROWING FROM THE PAST...
AND INTO THE FUTURE

Author and Environmental Educator

Terry O'Leary

"Terry O'Leary has done more for conservation in Ocean County than anyone I know." —Ted Gordon

Terry O'Leary grew up clamming and fishing on Raritan Bay and retains his love for the bayshore and the water. He founded and now serves as president of the Natural Resource Education Foundation of New Jersey, the nonprofit organization that manages the "Experience Barnegat Bay" program at the Lighthouse Center for Natural Resource Education in Waretown. When some of Terry's former students became involved with the fledgling Baymen's Museum, they called on their mentor, who subsequently became program director, publicist, grant-writer, and jack-of-all-trades to what would ultimately become the Tuckerton Seaport Museum.

After completing his studies at Montclair University and working for two years as a teacher in Newark, Terry earned a master's degree in environmental education from Glassboro State College (now Rowan University) in 1978. This led Terry to work with Dr. Eugene Vivian at the Conservation and Environmental Studies Center in Whitesbog. From that program in Whitesbog, comprised of highly selected individuals, came many of today's leading Pine Barrens environmental educators. Since 2000 Terry has been the education coordinator and resource interpretive specialist for the Forest Resource Education Center (FREC) in Jackson Township. "I'm a conservationist," he says about teaching that trees are a renewable resource, "but I've never been afraid of cutting trees and managing the forest, particularly to protect endangered species."

Terry was a founding member of the Forked River Mountain Coalition, a conservation group. According to co-founder Ted Gordon, "Terry O'Leary has done more for conservation in Ocean County than anyone I know." That's a well-deserved accolade for a man who has made a difference wherever he's gone.

Above: Saw-whet owl

Opposite: The Forest Resource Education Center at Jackson

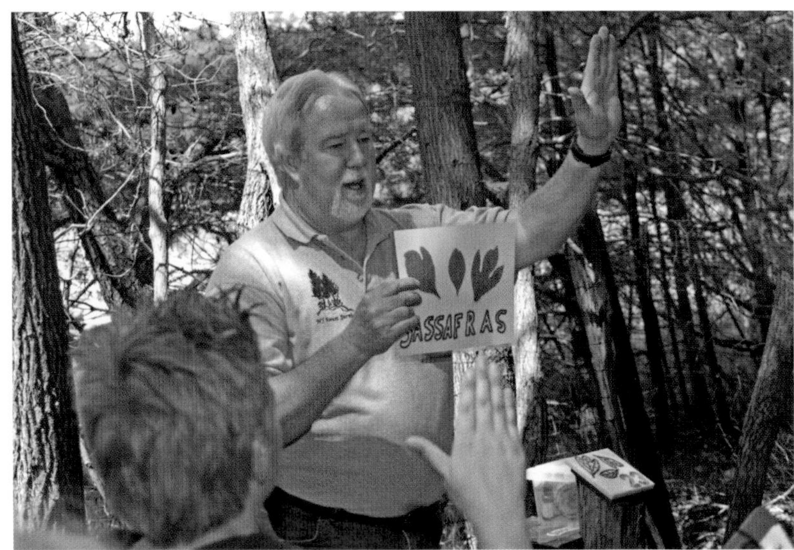

Terry teaches forest stewardship in a living outdoor classroom at the FREC.

Francesca Angiuoli, an educator at the FREC, with a visiting class

A young visitor at the FREC shakes hands with the Jersey Devil, a carving by Bob Moloughney.

Opposite: The Maritime Forest is one of the diverse habitats found at the Lighthouse Center in Waretown. At one time it stretched from Cape May to Sandy Hook and formed the transition zone between the Pine Barrens and the tide waters.

MARITIME FOREST
MARITIME FOREST
WHAT IS A MARITIME FOREST ?
• Proximity to the coast
• Soil Fertility from Marine Deposits
• Infrequent Forest Fires
• High Water Table
• Taller, more Luxuriant Foliage
• Tradition of Soil Amendments
clams & oyster shells, seaweed & eelgrass
• Coastal Climate
persistant wind, salt spray, tidal flooding
• History of Disturbance
lumbering, agriculture, grazing,
roadways, housing development
SOME CHARACTERISTIC SPECIES
TREES
Spanish Oak
Willow Oak
White Oak
Sweet Gum
Red Maple
Pitch Pine
Loblolly Pine
Red Cedar
American Holly
Hackberry
Gray Birch
Sassafras
Wild Black Cherry
Sour Gum
Swamp Magnolia
SHRUBS
Inkberry Holly
Bayberry
Marsh Elder
Highbush Blueberry
Sweet Pepperbush
Toothed Arrowood
Mountain Laurel
Beach Plum
Winterberry Holly
VINES
Greenbriar
Virginia Creeper
Poison Ivy
Fox Grape
Japanese Honeysuckle

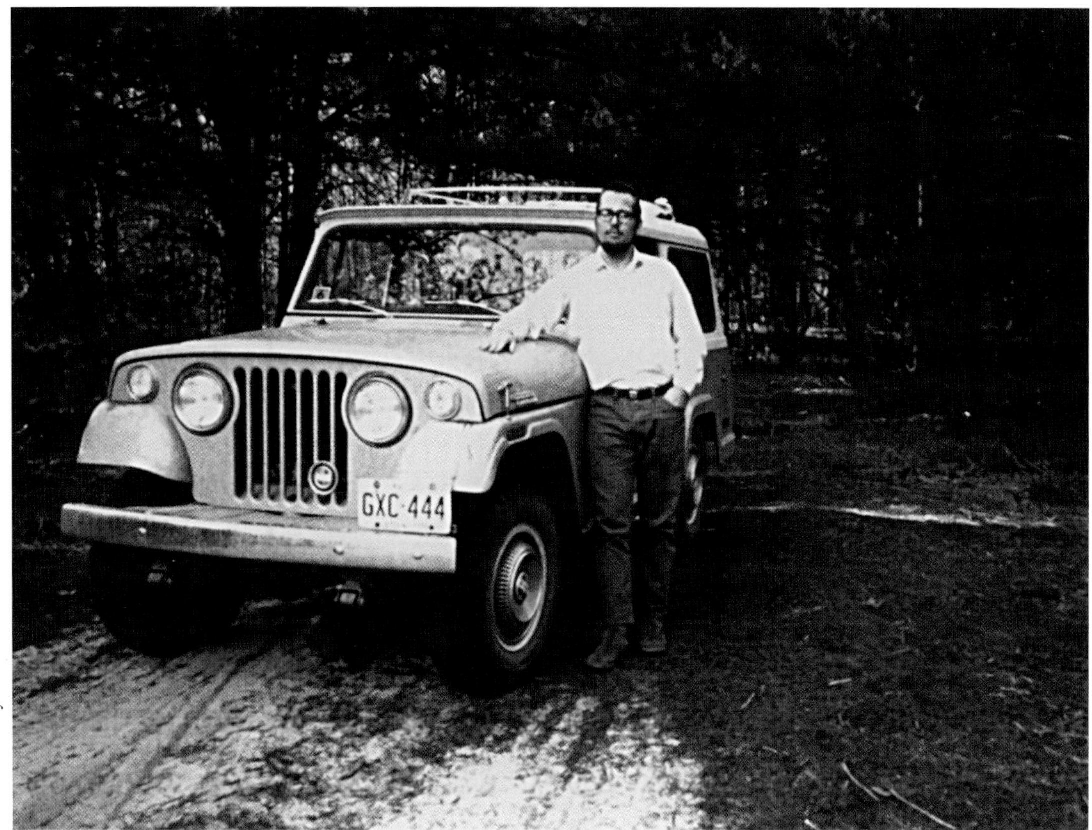

Photo courtesy of Ted Gordon

The Pine Barrens' Indiana Jones

If the New Jersey Pine Barrens has its own "Indiana Jones," it's Ted Gordon. In 1970, Ted bought a Jeep and, armed with topographical maps of the region, set out to pursue his goal of documenting and photographing all the historic sites within the Pine Barrens. An accomplished photographer, Ted's collection of more than 10,000 slides is a treasure trove of images, many of them showing historic sites that no longer exist. "I've always considered myself an explorer, a documenter, an educator, and a protector of rare species and old places," Ted explains.

Explorer and Educator

Ted Gordon

"I've driven every road in the Pine Barrens, from Monmouth to Cape May."

Ted Gordon's love affair with the Pine Barrens began when he was a boy, soon after he and his family moved to the U.S. from Germany. As early as age 11, he was venturing from his home near Fort Dix into the sandy pinewoods of Hanover Furnace and historic Whitesbog.

Ted is a historian and all-around naturalist, but is best known as one of the state's premiere botanists. He was president of the Philadelphia Botanical Club for 12 years and has led hundreds of workshops and field trips, introducing his beloved Pine Barrens to budding botanists and international plant scholars alike. Professionally, he has conducted scientific studies of natural areas in many parts of the Pinelands and is often called on to testify on behalf of preservation interests.

As a Pinelands Commissioner from 1998 to 2002, Ted was able to bring his extensive botanical knowledge to bear on several pressing conservation issues. He was instrumental in having the vanishing swamp-pink listed as an endangered species, and worked with Dr. David Fairbrothers to compile the original endangered plant list for the Pinelands Comprehensive Management Plan in 1980.

In 1987, Ted Gordon retired as a high school German and English teacher to devote all his energies to research, conservation, and teaching about the Pine Barrens. For the thousands of people who have been touched by his conviction and knowledge, that was a fateful decision.

Above: Bog asphodel

Ted surveys a field of bog asphodels, a threatened species in the Pine Barrens.

Evidence of the revenuer's axe makes a telltale outline in an old can used to hold the still's bounty.

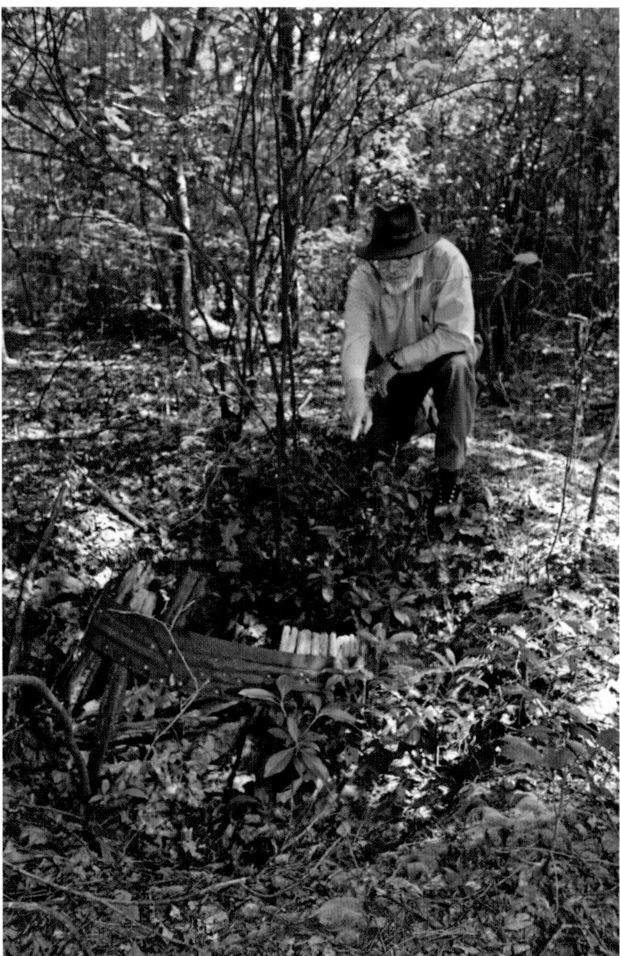

Ted at the site of a 1930s moonshiner's still in the Pines

Opposite: View from Forked River Mountain. Ted was a founding member of the coalition that preserved this key natural area.

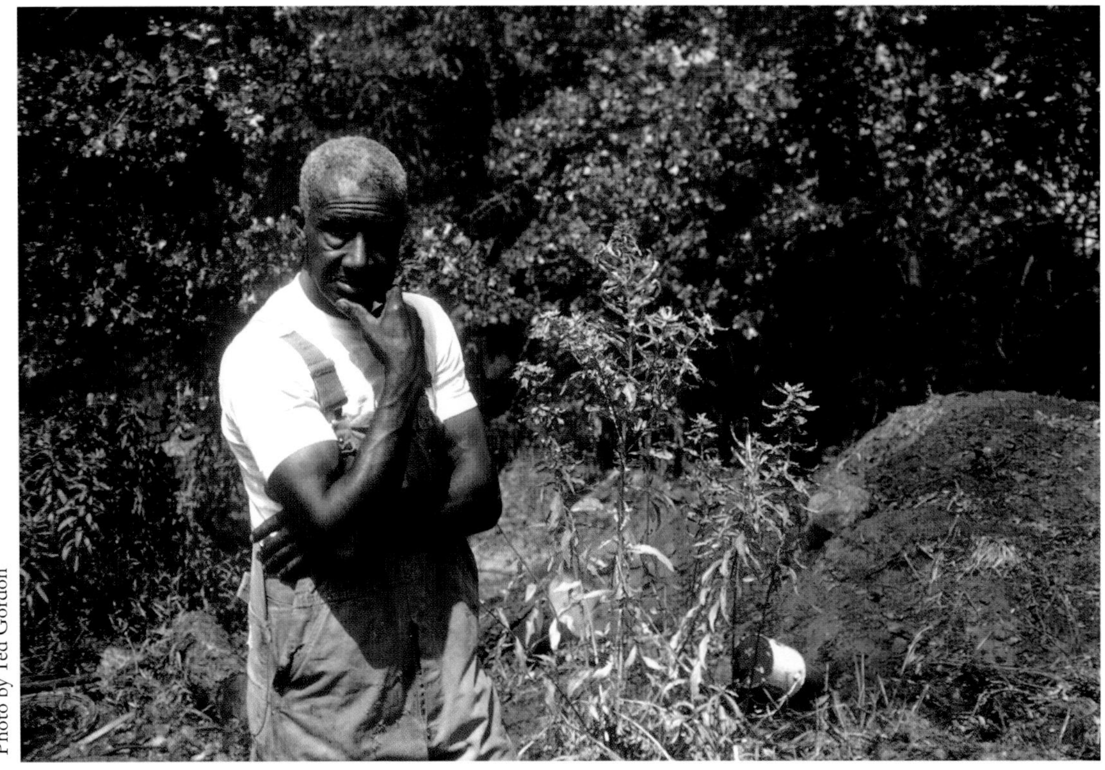

Photo by Ted Gordon

The Last of the Old Time Charcoal Makers

In 1974, on one of his Pine Barrens explorations, Ted Gordon came across Herbert Payne of Whiting making charcoal in the way of the old time colliers of the Pine Barrens. Until this time, it had been widely assumed that traditional charcoal making had died out by the early 1960s. According to Ted, "Many on the trail of a bit of romantic history have scanned the horizon for a wisp of gray smoke that might betray the location of a charcoal pit."

For two weeks, Ted observed, documented, and photographed Herbert Payne in the various operations of the open-pit coaling process. "I've burned coal in every conceivable way," Herbert once told Ted. Charcoal making was hard work, and the entire process took three weeks. Herbert's standard 12- to 14-cord feet of wood produced an average yield of 3 ½ tons or 350 bags of charcoal, which could bring in a total income of $612.50 when the market was buying. For Herbert, it was hard but honest work, and a labor of love that carried with it the satisfaction of knowing he was the last of a hardy breed.

Shortly before his death in 1980, Herbert Payne told Ted Gordon that the charcoal burn Ted had witnessed had been his last.

Opposite: Firing the pit (Photo by Ted Gordon)

Decoy Carver

Ray Nyman

"I knew what the ducks looked like and what I wanted."

Ray Nyman's roots in New Jersey go back nine generations to John Mathis. Mathis was one of the first European settlers in the Tuckerton area and the first European settler in the area surrounding the Bass River. It's no wonder then that Ray hews passionately to traditional decoy carving, a craft he says was pioneered by Native American hunters more than 10 centuries ago.

Decoy making is a true American art form, according to Ray, and his goal is to keep it alive. He carves by hand using old-time wood-carving tools and carefully chosen cedar slabs from a local Pinelands sawmill. The wood is dried and cured for more than a year before Ray draws a knife across it.

When Ray was discharged from the Navy in the 1960s, he built three Barnegat Bay sneakboxes, which are traditional Jersey duck boats, and began carving decoys. Since then, he estimates he has carved about 2,000 decoys. He has won more than 30 ribbons in shows for his ornamental decoys, but decoys carved specifically for hunting, known as gunning decoys, are his specialty.

Each area of the country has its own distinctive decoy style; Ray says Barnegat Bay decoys are on the small side, fashioned without keels, and hollowed out inside to make them lighter, allowing them to ride high in the water to limit freezing. Ray sells most of his decoys to hunters, carving grooved eyes for easy handling and smooth bodies so water and ice have no place to gather.

Today Ray lives in Marlton with his wife Barb, who is also a decoy carver. Together they showcase their craft at various historic and sporting events. Ray Nyman regularly presents old-style carving demonstrations at the Tuckerton Seaport Museum and at the Forest Education Resource Center, volunteering about 500 hours per year to educate people about his beloved folk art.

Above: Carving tools

Opposite: A 41-year-old broadbill decoy carved by Ray

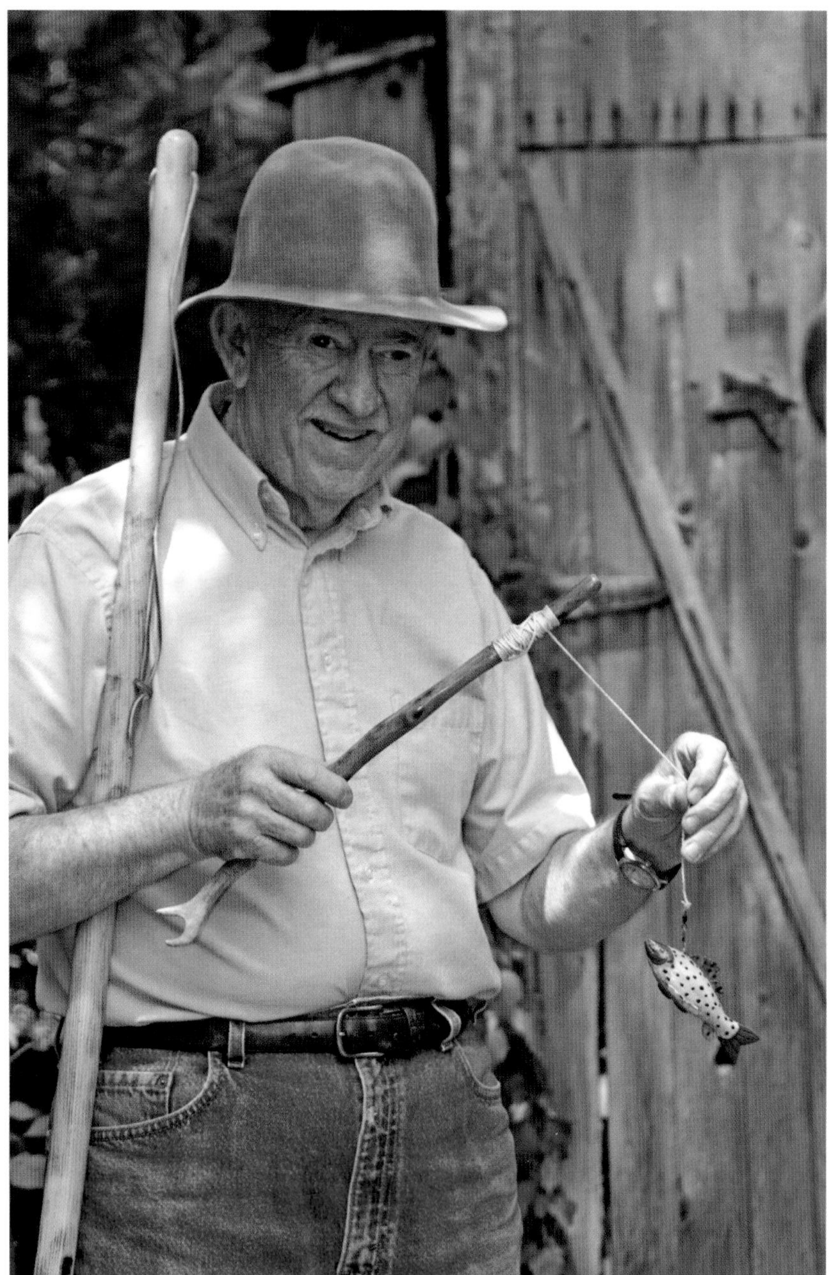
Ray displays one of his ice-fishing decoys he carved by hand with antique style tools.

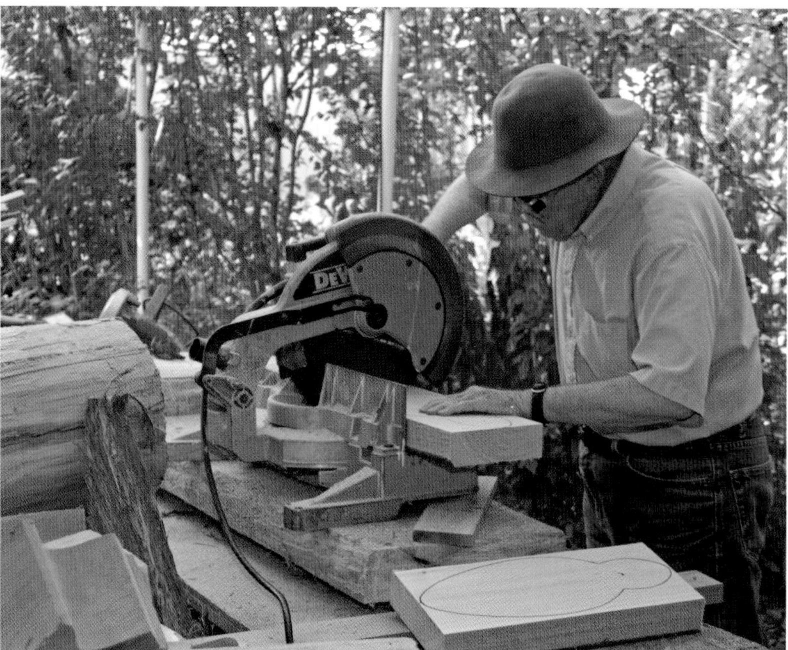

Ray uses a chopsaw to make the first rough cut in the Eastern cedar.

The carving of ice-fishing decoys is an early American folk art. The decoy shown above has copper fins and is filled with lead.

Opposite: Ray's working decoys and his handcarved recreation of a Barnegat Bay sneakbox.

Wildlife Rehabilitator

Jeanne Woodford

"My mother made me do it."

Jeanne Woodford, president of Woodford Cedar Run Wildlife Refuge, began a lifelong association with the Pine Barrens when her family purchased property in Medford in 1951. The Woodfords moved to Cedar Run when she was 13 and she's lived there ever since.

Jeanne's love of the Pines and dedication to its conservation was instilled by her mother, the late Elizabeth "Betty" Woodford, a renowned botanist and nature photographer. Betty taught Pinelands ecology courses at Lenape evening school and many of her students, including Ted Gordon, went on to become noted environmentalists.

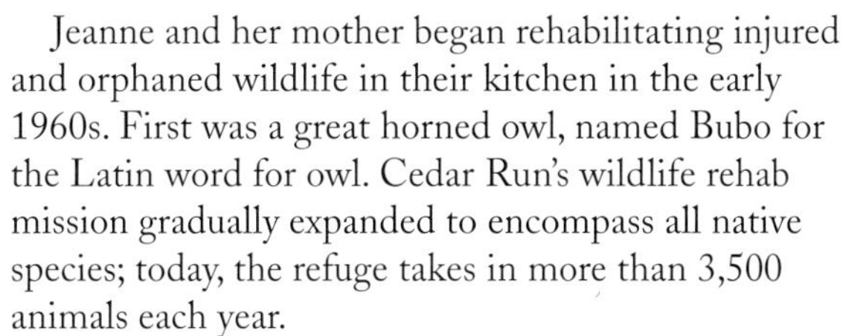

Jeanne and her mother began rehabilitating injured and orphaned wildlife in their kitchen in the early 1960s. First was a great horned owl, named Bubo for the Latin word for owl. Cedar Run's wildlife rehab mission gradually expanded to encompass all native species; today, the refuge takes in more than 3,500 animals each year.

"Habitat was most important to my mother," Jeanne emphasizes, and in 1998 she realized Betty's dream by successfully preserving Cedar Run through the New Jersey Green Acres Program. Although she jokes that "My mother made me do it," it was Jeanne's commitment that guaranteed the woodlands and wetlands at Cedar Run Lake will survive to be appreciated by future generations.

Jeanne taught elementary and special education in Moorestown for 27 years and recalls how her learning-disabled students bonded with the animals she brought into the classroom. She is passionate about the refuge's environmental education program, which serves nearly 20,000 children and adults each year.

As much as Jeanne Woodford enjoys traveling with her husband Fred Schwink, her heart is always at Cedar Run. "My mother worked here into her eighties," Jeanne says. Clearly, she expects to do the same.

Above: Aldora, a red-tailed hawk

Opposite: Terri Loy, Education Director at the refuge, introduces Aldora to a visiting class of schoolchildren.

Grey, an Eastern screech-owl, was hit by a car and suffered brain damage.

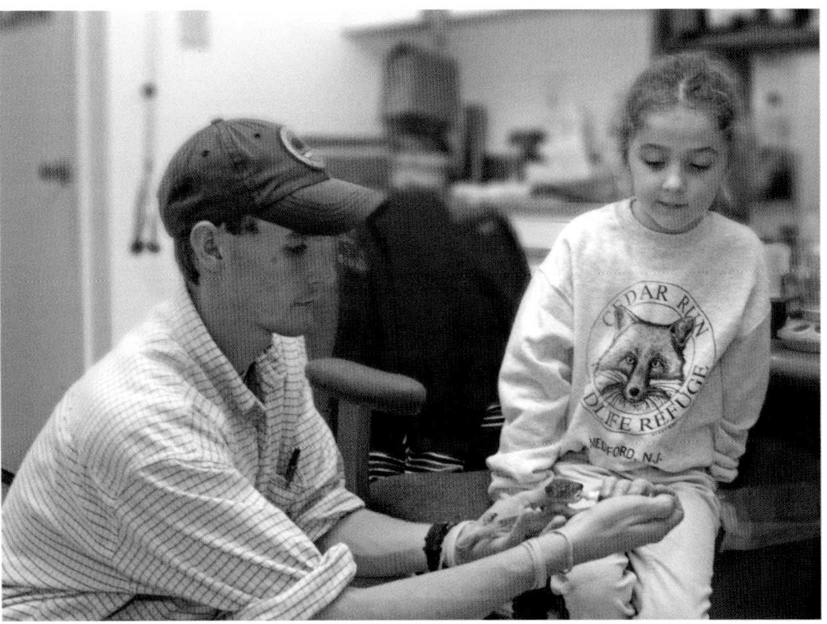

At the Woodford Cedar Run Wildlife Refuge, a young visitor watches staff member Bradley Angel feed a newborn squirrel.

Clack, an Eastern screech-owl, had surgery for a severe impact injury.

Shadow, a gray fox, had become habituated to humans by a pet owner and can no longer live in the wild.

A Virginia rail bird is rehabilitated at the refuge.

Orion, a bald eagle, was injured when he flew into high tension wires and is now unable to fly free.

Photo by Joseph Volk

"I think mankind needs wilderness in his life to enjoy and appreciate and to know that it's a part of what has always been there." —Elizabeth Woodford

Elizabeth and James Woodford founded Cedar Run Wildlife Refuge in 1957 on 184 acres of land they purchased in Medford. Over the next 40 years, they devoted their lives to Pinelands preservation, environmental education, and wildlife rehabilitation. Betty became an expert botanist, naturalist, nature

photographer, and wildlife rehabilitator. Jim, a teacher, spent his spare time building enclosures, repairing fences, and keeping the operation running. Today, Cedar Run staff and board members continue Betty and Jim's work, led by their daughter Jeanne, who is the refuge's president.

Conservationist and Birder

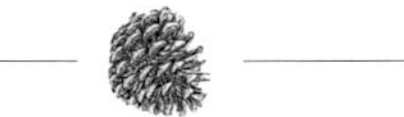

Janet Jackson-Gould

"I'm still learning."

Janet Jackson-Gould is a lifelong Burlington County resident whose early impressions of the Pine Barrens were formed during trips to the shore. "It wasn't till years later that I realized what an ecological and historical treasure they are."

When her children were young, Janet volunteered as docent at the Philadelphia Zoo. There she developed an interest in birds, which led her to the New Jersey Audubon Society. She was elected to the Audubon board in the mid-1970s, serving for nearly 20 years, three of them as president. Audubon Society field trips sparked her interest in both the natural and human history of the Pines.

In 1979, Janet joined the Pine Barrens Coalition, a group that was fighting to save the Pines from rampant development and a proposed jetport. Along with Nan Hunter-Walnut, Mae Barringer, Elmer Rowley, and many others, she wrote letters, lobbied politicians, testified at legislative hearings, and attended rallies. Once the Pinelands Preservation Acts were passed, she worked with a team of environmentalists to include strong protective elements in the Comprehensive Management Plan.

Life took a new turn when Janet remarried. She and her husband Bruce "Bear" Gould purchased a farm in Tabernacle in 1992 and went into the Clydesdale business. Over the next several years, the Goulds bred more than a dozen foals and used a team of geldings to pull wagons for weddings, festivals, and parades.

Janet began volunteering at Woodford Cedar Run Wildlife Refuge in Medford in 1996, and when Bruce passed away in 1999, she became executive director. She retired in 2006, but her interest in the Pines remains a driving force in her life. "I'm still learning," she smiles.

Above: A rose-breasted grosbeak

Opposite: Janet and two of the Clydesdales that she and her husband bred

Sawyer

Ed McCay

"I'll probably be the one to cut the last standing cedar in the woods."

Ed McCay has harvested Atlantic white cedar from Pine Barrens swamps for more than 40 years. He cuts the timber at his own sawmill, tucked away on 70 acres in Nesco, Mullica Township. He also farms 40 acres of blueberries and is restoring a 1780 farmhouse on the property that runs along an old stagecoach route.

Ed was born in Medford and grew up in Tabernacle, and represents the fourth generation of his family to wrest a living from the Pine Barrens. He followed the "Piney cycle" in his youth, collecting pine balls, harvesting sphagnum moss, hunting, and picking blueberries and cranberries in season. On Saturday nights he often traveled with his banjo to George and Joe Albert's "Home Place" near Waretown to play with other musicians.

As an employee of the New Jersey State Park System, Ed ran the historic sawmill at Batsto for 10 years. He possesses an abiding respect and appreciation for Piney culture and, in particular, the role that sawmills have played in the region, and has always enjoyed sharing his knowledge and passion for the topic.

Ed is a regular at events such as the annual Pine Barrens Jamboree at Wells Mills Park, where he sells his cut timber to decoy carvers and boat builders. He also supplies cedar fence posts to order.

"It's getting harder to find wood to cut," according to Ed. "The state owns most of it and getting permits is a long process." Nevertheless, he says he will persevere "to the last cedar."

Above: The sign that welcomes visitors to Ed's "Place in the Woods"

Opposite: Ed's sawmill

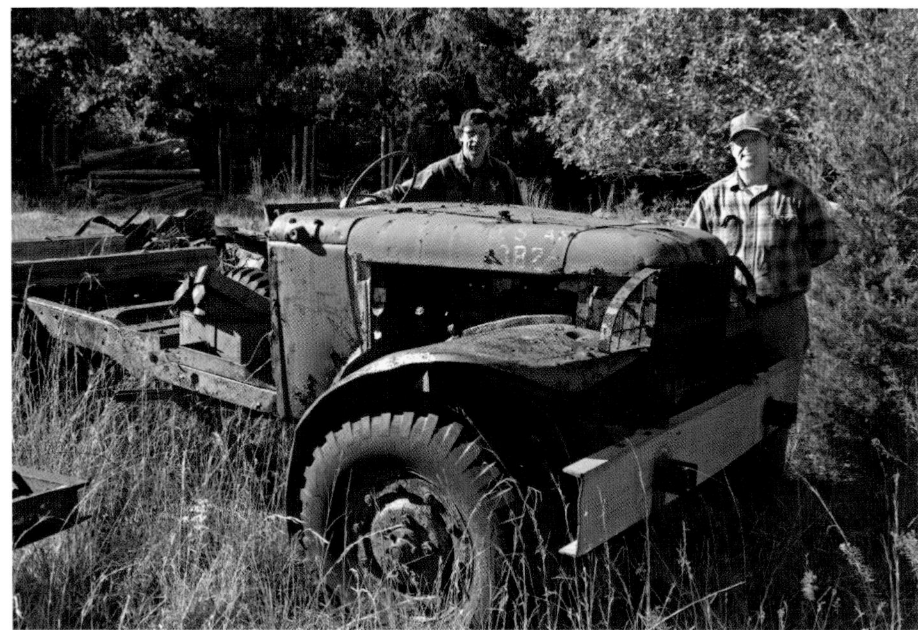

Ed (right) and Scott Kozar, who works with Ed, stand beside an old munitions carrier that they use to haul cut timber out of the woods.

Ed measures the cut of the log.

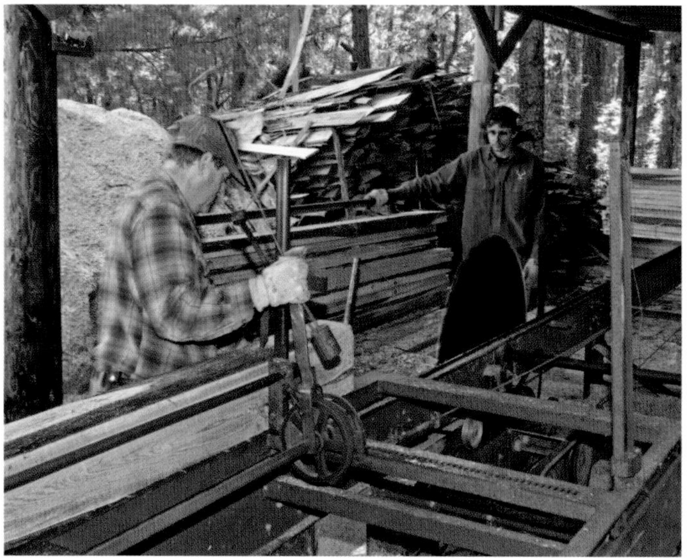

Ed and Scott at work

Opposite: An Atlantic white cedar swamp in the Forked River Mountains area

Trapper

Jack Vanaman

"I don't think the muskrat population will ever come back to its peak."

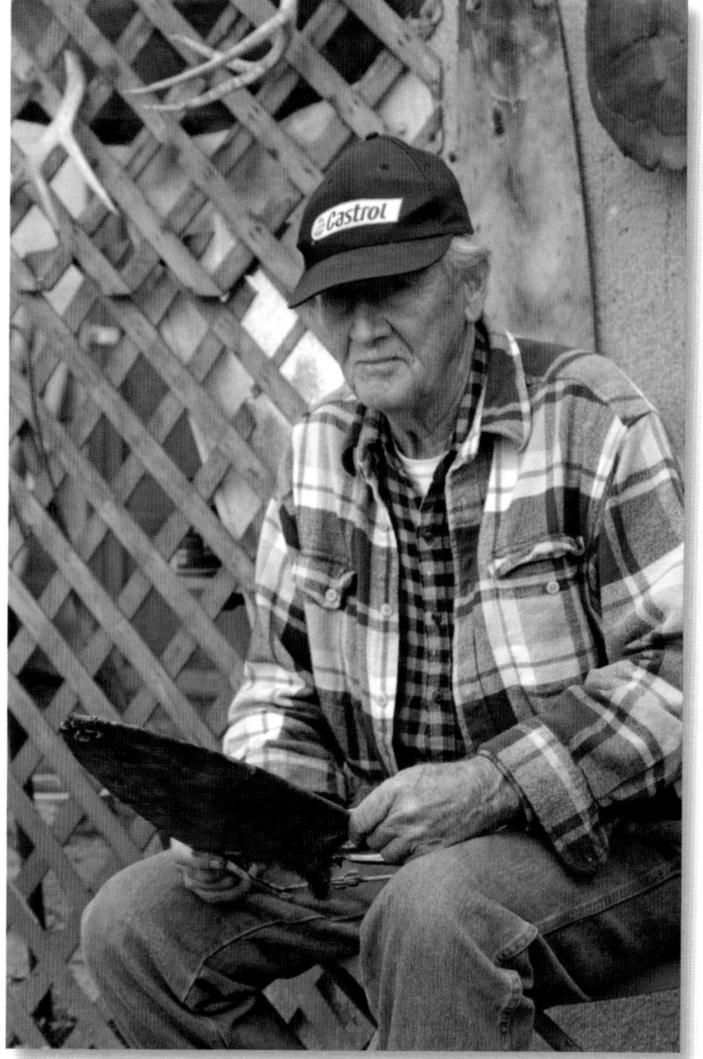

Jack Vanaman was born in Smithville in 1931 and has been a skilled bayman all his life. His father drowned in a Nor'easter while oystering when Jack was 10 years old, leaving young Jack and his brother to earn a living by trapping, catching snapping turtles, clamming, and gill-netting.

Jack joined the Army at age 16 and served in Korea. When he returned from the conflict, he went to work as a bridge operator for the state, retiring 29 years later as chief operator. Having trapped and fished his entire life, he took to trapping full time when he retired.

Muskrats taken from the Mullica River are prime and much sought after, according to Jack. A relatively large variety, they have red fur underneath and their pelts are of high quality. "When the market was good, the buyers would break your door down to get the local furs," he claims. He recalls the best stretch of trapping he ever had was a two-day period in which he caught 102 muskrats for the Canadian fur market.

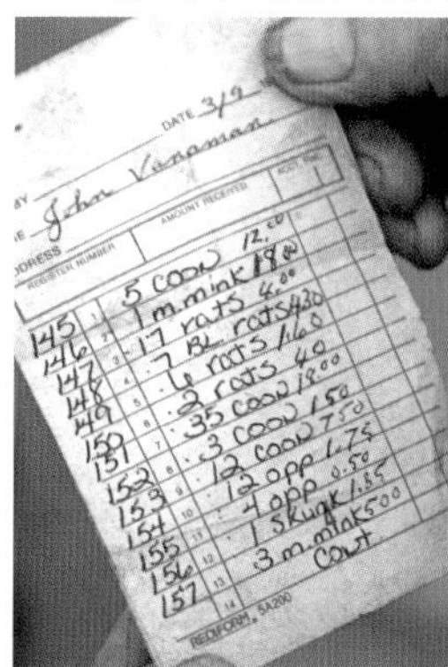
DATE 3/9
John Vanaman
5 coon
1 m. mink
17 rats
7 BL rats
6 rats
2 rats
35 coon
3 coon
12 coon
12 opp
4 opp
1 skunk
3 m. mink
REDIFORM 5A200

Jack thinks that natural predation from hawks, eagles, foxes, and raccoons is having a bigger impact on the muskrat population than trapping. Phragmites, a non-native reed, has overgrown the marshes and is crowding out the muskrats' natural food supply. The thick reeds also make it difficult to reach the muskrat houses.

Jack Vanaman's outdoor skills earned him the coveted Hurley Conklin Award in 2006. The Ocean County Parks and Recreation Department present this award to "People who have lived their lives in the Barnegat Bay tradition." However, the muskrat pelts that once brought more than $10 are now fetching only $4 and the future "doesn't look too good." Jack still gets up and goes out to the marsh, though, following the way of life he loves.

Above: A receipt from a fur auction

Opposite: Jack stands atop a muskrat house in the marsh.

Racoon furs flank a snapping turtle shell on the wall as Jack prepares to hang his muskrat furs out to dry.

Jack builds many of his own diving traps.

Jack's homemade snapping turtle trap

A Conibear trap, which is used for muskrats

Opposite: Jack sets a muskrat trap.

CHATSWORTH GENERAL STORE
"Buzby's"
CHATSWORTH GENERAL STORE
"Buzby's"
3959
CHESHI
CAT
609 894-441
BOOKS
FINE ART
CRAFTS•GIFTS

Storekeeper and Author

Marilyn Schmidt

"People ask, 'Where are the Pineys?'
I tell them, right here!"

Historic Buzby's General Store in Chatsworth stood vacant for seven years until Marilyn Schmidt happened by during a cranberry festival. She fell in love with the landmark building and its history, and in 1996 she purchased the assignment of the tax lien and foreclosed on banks and others holding an interest in it. Marilyn's dream and ambition was to restore this Pine Barrens icon to its former prominence.

Even before moving to Chatsworth, Marilyn had begun to immerse herself in the legend and lore of the Pine Barrens from her home base in Barnegat Light. She has since become a knowledgeable local historian who loves to hear stories of bygone days from old-timers who visit Buzby's. Among the more than 20 books and booklets she has written are guides to the Pinelands, plus numerous cookbooks and gardening titles, all published by Pine Barrens Press—a division of Marilyn's Barnegat Light Press.

An old-fashioned country store atmosphere prevails in Buzby's. Today, as a Pinelands Resource Center, it specializes in books and crafts of the Pine Barrens. Marilyn also provides a retail outlet for local artists, crafters, and weavers. Pumpkin, the resident cat, presides over the premises and may rank among the most photographed cats in the state.

Marilyn is a pharmacologist and ghostwriter, as well as an author, artist, publisher, historian, and master gardener. Thanks to her vision, determination, and hard work, historic Buzby's is once again a gathering place where old-timers and travelers can mingle and swap stories in the "Capital of the Pines." Today the store is listed on the New Jersey and National Register of Historic Places.

Above: One of Marilyn's many books

Opposite: Chatsworth General Store

Photo courtesy of Marilyn Schmidt

Buzby's store circa 1920

A replica of the original outhouse

Buzby's General Store

Designated an historic site, Buzby's General Store in Chatsworth was built in 1865 and has been a Pine Barrens social and cultural center throughout its history. From 1897 until 1937, Willis Jefferson Buzby and his wife Myrtle, who were known affectionately as the "King and Queen of the Pineys," ran the store. After Willis's death, his son Willis Jonathan Buzby (Jack) inherited the store, along with the title, "King of the Pineys." Jack sold the store in 1967. Since then, various owners have operated the store.

The Buzbys operated a traditional country store, selling everything from groceries and home goods to building supplies and gasoline. For a time the store also served as the local post office. Located on Route 563 (a popular route between Philadelphia and the Jersey shore), Buzby's now houses Marilyn Schmidt's delightful gift and bookshop that celebrates the enduring traditions of the Pines.

The restored general store in Chatsworth

The store has a warm and welcoming environment for visitors to the "Capital of the Pines."

Last of the Carranza Recoverers

Albertus V. Pepper

"Dwelling on the past will only subordinate your happy future."

Midwife "Lib" Hart brought Albertus V. Pepper into this world in 1912. Albertus spent most of his adult life in Chatsworth, "the Capital of the Pines," and held various jobs with the Jersey Central Railroad and county road crews until he saved enough money to purchase a blueberry farm south of Chatsworth. The farm remains in the family and today is worked by his son, Albertus Jr.

Albertus is associated with one of the most well known events in Pine Barrens history, the fatal crash of Emilio Carranza, the "Mexican Lindbergh." During the night of July 12, 1928, Albertus recalls hearing the sound of Carranza's Ryan B-1 monoplane during a thunderstorm. The next day a local blueberry picker discovered Carranza's body and plane. He raced back to Chatsworth and reported his findings. Albertus and a group of local pineys went into the woods and recovered the flyer's body and remnants of the plane. Albertus claims to be the last surviving member of that recovery team.

The Carranza recovery may be what Albertus is most famous for, but it's not what he is most proud of: He is the longest-living member of the United Methodist Church in Chatsworth. The beautiful, knotty pine wood that graces the interior of the church was harvested in the nearby woods by Albertus and fellow parishioners, and milled in Chatsworth. The all-volunteer renovation was completed in April 1956.

Not content merely to be associated with these two historic events in Chatsworth's history, Albertus served as the township's mayor throughout the 1950s. In recent years, he can often be found on the front porch of Buzby's General Store, visiting with his good friend Marilyn Schmidt, eating hot dogs, and fondly recalling bygone times in this historic Pine Barrens community.

Above: A fallen Aztec eagle emblem on the Carranza Memorial in Tabernacle

Opposite: Inside the United Methodist Church in Chatsworth

The United Methodist Church in Chatsworth was built in 1875 as a Presbyterian church. It was hit by lightning in 1893 and destroyed by fire. After it was rebuilt in 1899, it became a Methodist church. In 1984 the stained glass windows were handcrafted by a local Chatsworth artisan, Gedi Gadauskas, who owned Buzby's General Store for a period of time. The birds, plants, and animals crafted on the windows are all native to the Pine Barrens.

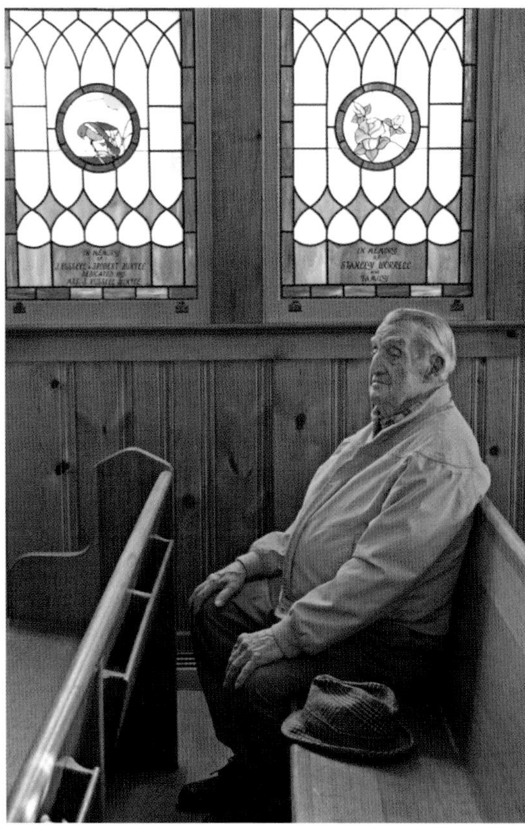

Albertus is the oldest living member of the church congregation.

Albertus and Marilyn Schmidt enjoy a chat on the porch of Buzby's.

Carranza Memorial

Emilio Carranza

Deep within Wharton State Forest, set back from the little traveled Carranza Road and just along a stretch of the Batona Trail, stands a 12-foot-high stone monument dedicated to the fallen aviator, Emilio Carranza Rodriguez—the "Lone Eagle of Mexico." The monument was erected in 1933 and paid for by contributions of pesos from the children of Mexico. The image of an Aztec eagle is carved on one side of the monument while the other offers a dedication to "Captain aviator Emilio Carranza, muerto tragicamente el 12 de Julio 1928."

Captain Carranza's single-engine monoplane crashed in the Pine Barrens near Tabernacle during a severe thunderstorm while on the return leg of a goodwill flight between Mexico City and New York.

The following day near Sandy Ridge, John Henry Carr, a resident of Chatsworth who was out picking berries with his mother and sister, found a piece of an aircraft wing. It was from Carranza's plane and soon after the discovery the aviator's death was confirmed. Carr, who also claimed to have found Carranza's body, reported that the pilot was holding a flashlight in his hand.

Carranza was taken from the crash scene to Chatsworth and placed in the garage in the rear of Willis Jefferson Buzby's store. According to Willis's daughter-in-law Kathryn "Katie" Buzby, "Rescuers brought Carranza's body out of the woods and they placed the pilot on my mother-in-law's wallpapering board." Next the body was transported to Mount Holly where it was draped with an American flag from American Legion Post 11 and taken by train to Mexico. Today the flag hangs in Mexico's School of Aviation. Over the years, members of Legion Post 11 have traveled to Mexico and met with members of Carranza's family.

Beginning in 1929, a year after Carranza's death, and continuing uninterrupted to this day, the Mount Holly Legionnaires have conducted a memorial service at the monument on the second Saturday in July. It has become a festive occasion attended by locals, the aviator's descendants, Mexican diplomats, Scout troops, and, of course, the Legionnaires.

Captain Carranza's mission was a goodwill flight to the U.S., in appreciation of a similar gesture Charles Lindbergh had made some months earlier when he flew nonstop from Washington, DC to Mexico City. The two aviators met during Lindbergh's trip and became fast friends; both flew Ryan B-1 monoplanes, and to this day Carranza is often referred to by those on both sides of the border as "Mexico's Lindbergh."

The memory of Captain Emilio Carranza, his mission of friendship between neighboring countries, and his legendary courage continue to be an inspiration for citizens of both Mexico and the U.S. In retrospect and in ways the fallen aviator could not have imagined, his mission succeeded, and he will always hold a special place in Pine Barrens history.

WILDLIFE

Homesteader

Lillian Hoey Gomez

"Gosh, what more could I ask for? I have the best of everything."

Lillian Hoey Gomez recalls, "Barnegat was the perfect town to be born in during 1945. All the kids on the block went barefoot, trailed through the woods, and brought home turtles and snakes." "With that as my background, the perfect job opportunity presented itself. I was on a canoe trip with an Ocean County Parks recreation leader. He was resting under a tree when I asked how he got his job. 'Applied for it,' he replied. So the next day I applied for it—and I got it!"

"From then on I was leading groups of unsuspecting followers through the forest on beaver stalks, rare flower hunts, canoe trips, van tours of lost towns, owl prowls, and, best of all, Jersey Devil hunts."

From 1993 to 2002, Lillian was asked to interview baymen and women who participated in the annual Ocean County Decoy and Gunning show. Because she was a Piney, they relaxed and shared their best stories of life on the bay and on the land.

This chapter in her life ended when Lillian retired in 2002. She and her husband Henry bought the Swamp Fox Sportsmen's Gun Club, which sits on 22 pinewoods acres between the two tributaries of the Bass River. The remote cabin, deep in the woods down a long sugar-sand road, had been in disrepair from years of nonuse.

The area is a naturalist's paradise, known for its many rare and endangered animal and plant species, including the elusive curly-grass fern. "Every day we sit at our table and are treated to dinner theater," Lillian smiles. "Deer and rabbits come to dine on the clover, grey and red foxes feed on leftover bird seed, and raccoons raid the hummingbird feeder."

Above: White-tail doe

Opposite: The Gomez homestead

Curly-grass fern

Indian-pipe plant

Striped wintergreen

Pink lady's-slipper

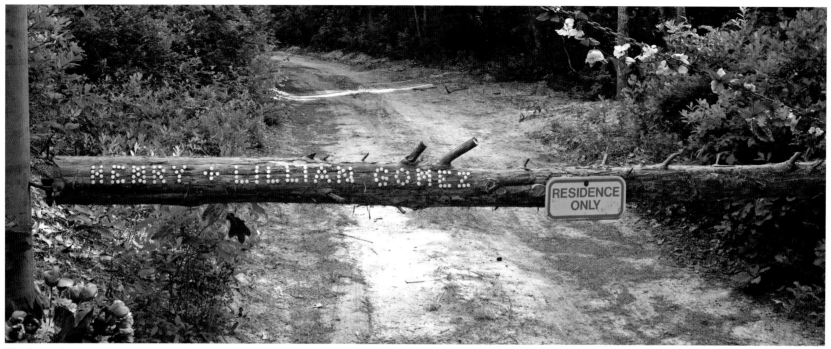

The Gomez's 22-acre property in the Pines is a hunter's and a naturalist's paradise that includes a forest stream, rare plants, and Henry's own skeet range.

Entomologist and Author

Howard Boyd

"My particular interest has been tiger beetles, and I have studied and worked with these interesting critters for well over fifty years."

Howard P. Boyd made his first trip to the Pine Barrens in pursuit of insects in 1938. He's been in and out of the Pines ever since—collecting, studying, photographing, teaching, and writing about all aspects of its nature and ecology.

Born in the Boston area, Howard grew up on two small suburban farms. He won a wildflower contest in the eighth grade, earned every nature merit badge in the Boy Scout Handbook, and went on to earn a degree in biological sciences from Boston University with an emphasis in botany. He would later return to college and add a degree in entomology.

Howard married his high school sweetheart Doris Fowler in 1938 and began a 31-year career with the Boy Scouts of America. An entomologist who ranks among the world's leading experts on tiger beetles, he was editor of *Entomological News* from 1974 to 2003 and served as president of the American Entomological Society from 1977 to 1981.

Along with Doris, a gifted nature photographer in her own right, Howard retired in 1969 to build a home in the Pines. He was soon teaching at Whitesbog as an adjunct professor for Glassboro State College (now Rowan University) and lecturing at Burlington County College. He has found time to serve on the board of the New Jersey Audubon Society and the Pinelands Preservation Alliance, and provided leadership within many other environmental organizations.

Thousands have come to know Howard through his books about the Pine Barrens. He wrote his first book, *A Field Guide to the Pine Barrens of New Jersey*, when he was in his mid-70s and has written three more since, including his forthcoming book on Pine Barrens ecology. Now in his 90s, Howard Boyd can still be found hiking through the Pines for his entomology projects and book research.

Above: Ox beetles

Opposite: Howard working his pitfall trap

Tiger beetle

Howard examines the material in the trap.

Howard sets the traps.

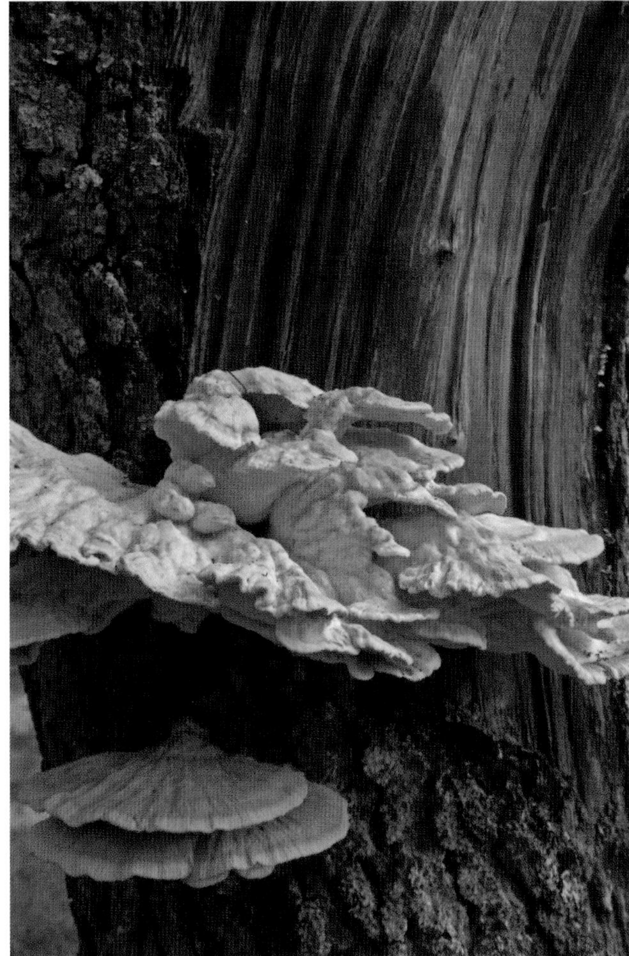

Artist's Fungus (described below by Howard Boyd in *A Field Guide to the Pine Barrens of New Jersey*)

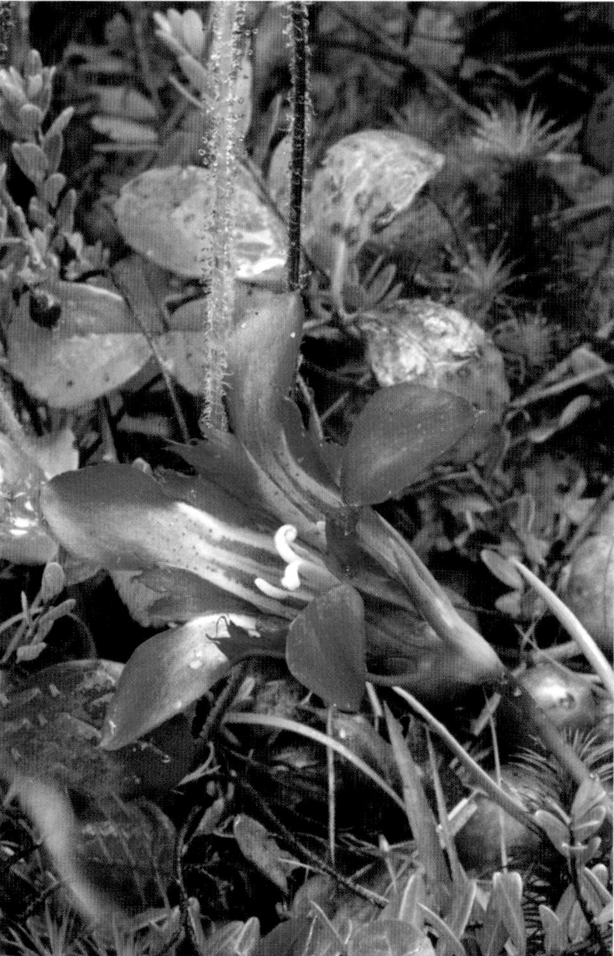

Pine-barren Gentian (described below by Howard Boyd in *A Field Guide to the Pine Barrens of New Jersey*)

Bracket or Artist's Fungus *Fomes applanatum*

Generally fan-shaped, shelf-like, woody fungus that grows on the sides of trunks of hardwood trees, notably oaks. The upper surface is hard and zoned. The undersurface is smooth and white (when fresh), on which picures may be drawn. This fungus is a favorite habitat of the forked fungus beetle. (Howard P. Boyd 1991, 79)

Pine-barren Gentian *Gentiana autumnalis* 6" - 1 1/2'

Stem slender, simple or occasionally branched. Leaves opposite, very narrow, linear, long, up to 2". Flowers solitary or up to 2-3, at tops of stems or branches, large, 5 widely spreading lobes from deep, tubular corolla, bright, light ultramarine blue, brown-speckled inside corolla. An endangered species found in moist, open, sandy barrens, bogs, in heart of pines. Flowers September-early October. (Howard P. Boyd 1991, 198)

“I’m glad that I grew up in the time that I did.”

Forest Fire Observer

Eileen Bethanis

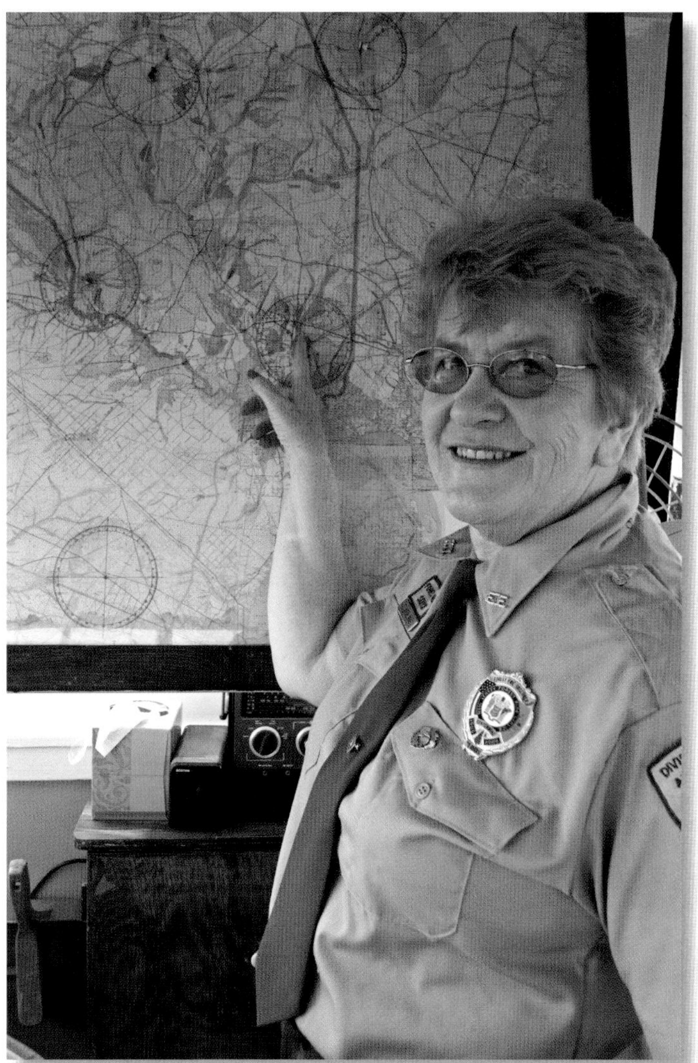

Eileen Bethanis has spent a lifetime fighting fire. She was born in Lower Bank, where her family roots go back nine generations. In 1975 she joined the volunteer fire department in Lower Bank, eventually rising to the rank of captain at a time when women firefighters were a rarity.

For 22 years, Eileen climbed a forest fire tower each morning to scan the horizon for smoke. Fifteen of those years were with the New Jersey Forest Fire Service, as the only full-time female fire observer in the state. A graduate of the Atlantic County Fire Academy, she fought fires in the woods as well as in town.

Eight-hour shifts on the fire tower were split between periods of boredom, high anxiety during electrical storms, and swift action when a fire was spotted in the Pinelands. Inside Eileen’s observation room at the top of the tower, temperatures ranged from 40°F in the winter to over 100°F in summer months. Each day she surveyed the forest floor to record temperature and humidity, data used to predict how quickly a fire might spread.

Eileen met her late husband Art while working for the Forest Fire Service. Art was also a forest fire observer and, although their fire towers were 14 miles apart and beyond the range of their portable radios, they signaled each other by reflecting sunlight off shiny objects.

Eileen Bethanis recently retired to the house in Barnegat that Art built for her. Barnegat keeps her close to her beloved Pine Barrens and sustains her memories of a lifetime of adventure and service as a pioneer firefighter.

Above: A long climb up for 22 years

Opposite: Eileen scans the horizon from the tower for evidence of fire.

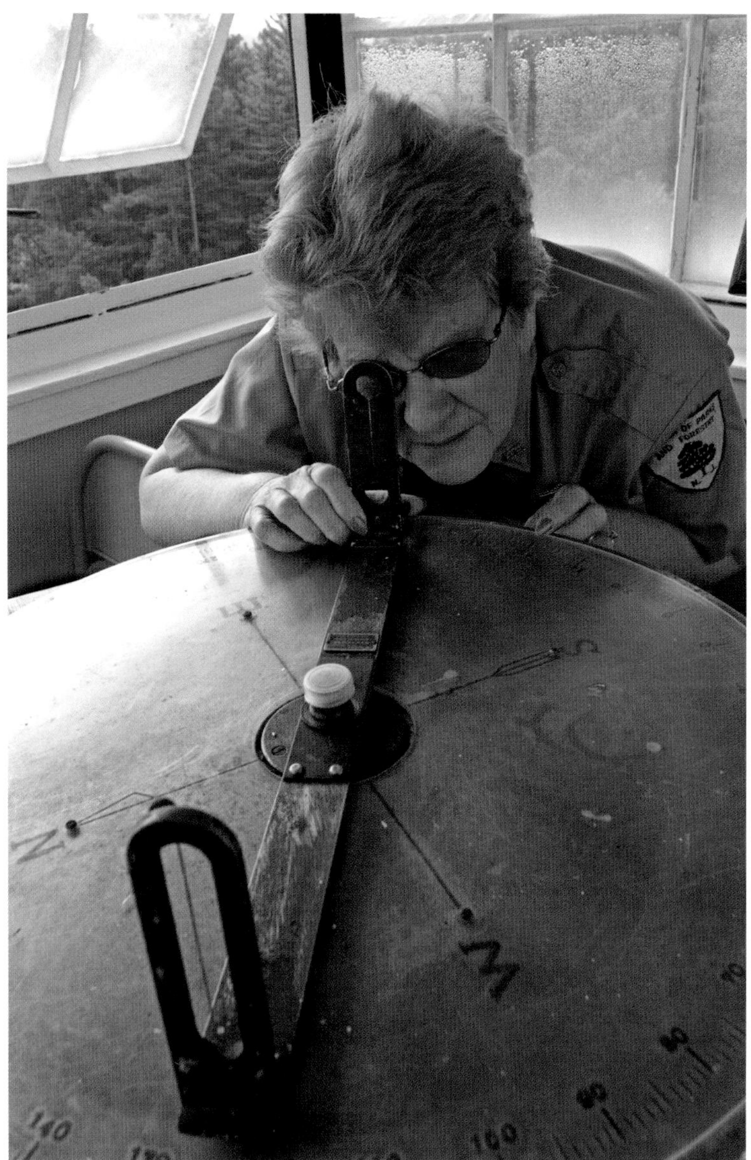

Eileen uses an alidade to determine the horizontal bearing of a forest fire. Two or more towers are needed to triangulate the location of a fire.

The fire tower at Apple Pie Hill today

Photo courtesy of the New Jersey Forest Fire Service

A 1908 photo of one of New Jersey's first fire towers, constructed in Woodmansie for $10

Photo courtesy of the New Jersey Forest Fire Service

The Four Mile tower was constructed in 1910.

Photo by Walter Bien, PhD

Fire in the Pines

Simply stated, the Pine Barrens, as we know it today, needs fire to survive. This is because the high heat of wildfires causes pitch pine cones to pop open and distribute their seeds. Without periodic high-intensity fires, oaks would eventually take over and crowd out the pines. The unique ecosystem in the Pine Barrens that fosters its array of plant and animal species would be changed forever. This is already occurring to a significant extent as the increasing number of residential areas being built on the perimeter of the Pine Barrens requires the NJ Forest Fire Service to focus on fire prevention and suppression.

To prevent and control widespread, destructive fires, fire wardens conduct low-intensity ground fires referred to as "controlled" or "prescribed" burns each year beginning in November. By burning off the forest's ground cover, the fire wardens prevent wildfires from using this cover as fuel when the fire season starts in the spring. This goes a long way toward minimizing the spread of uncontrolled wildfires and protecting the people and property of the area. However, according to Howard Boyd in *A Field Guide to the Pine Barrens of New Jersey*, "Lack of high intensity wildfires and crown fires have an adverse effect on plant diversity and in maintaining the traditional balance of vegetation in the Pinelands, principally between the pines and oaks."

The challenge facing the Forest Fire Service is in addressing the needs of public safety through educational programs, fire prevention, and controlled burns, while at the same time preserving the ecological integrity of the Pine Barrens. It's a delicate balancing act that puts the men and women of the Forest Fire Service at the forefront of efforts to preserve the Pinelands for generations to come.

“Hand picking cranberries,
now that’s a job you don’t want to do!”

Emil Brown is nearly 90 now and resides outside the Pine Barrens he loves so well. Not long ago, he returned to Hog Wallow for a visit to the family homestead he left in 1990. The cedar cabin he was born in is but a shell of what it was, and is slowly being reclaimed by the forest. Emil lived most of his life here along with his father Fred Brown, who was made famous by John McPhee in *The Pine Barrens.*

In the surrounding woods and fields, Emil worked the traditional cycle of the seasons. Like his father and grandfather before him, he raked sphagnum moss in spring, picked “sweet huckleberries” in summer, scooped cranberries in fall (“Now *that’s* a job you don’t want to do!”), and cut cordwood in winter. For a time, he also worked on a road crew, a job he refers to as “engineering the roads.”

Fred Brown was the great-grandson of Zechariah Jenkins, for whom the hamlets of Jenkins and Jenkins Neck were named. Fred married Elizabeth Mick and they raised seven children, including Emil, first in Jenkins and then in the homestead at Hog Wallow near Fred’s cranberry bogs and blueberry fields.

Emil was the only one of the children to remain at Hog Wallow after Fred’s death. For years he followed the old way of life, moving from one seasonal job to another. On Saturday nights you could often find him at Albert Hall in Waretown, singing and playing his guitar with the Muddy Mountain Blue Grass Boys.

Emil Brown may no longer live in the Pines, but he is as much a part of this world as its endless sandy roads, cool cedar swamps, and slow-moving streams.

Above: Emil meets Bob Heritage, an old friend, along the road.

Opposite: In 2006, Emil returns to the old homestead.

Piney

Emil Brown

Photo by Shailendra Jain, 1994

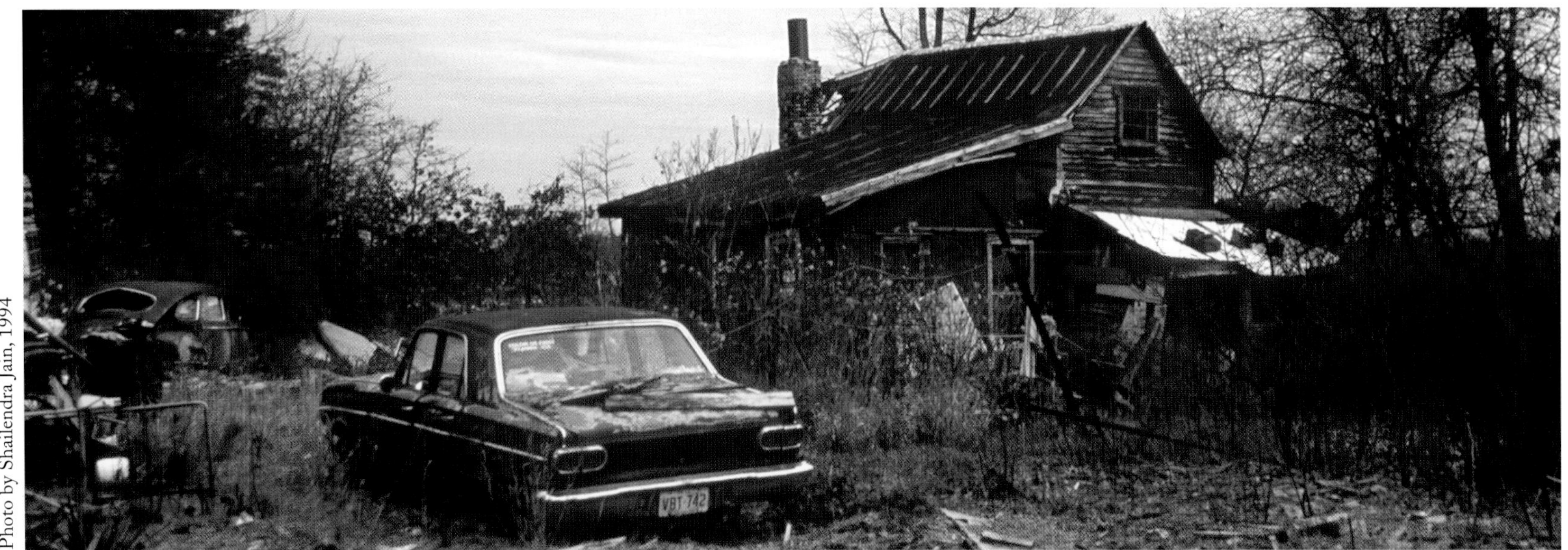

Old cars have long littered the yard at the Brown homestead, even when it was occupied. In his book, John McPhee recounts a discussion with Fred Brown, Emil's father. "I asked Fred what all those cars were doing in his yard, and he said that one of them was in running condition and the rest were its predecessors. The working vehicle was a 1956 Mercury. Each of the seven others had at one time or another been his best car, and each, in turn, had lain down like a sick animal and had died right there in the yard, unless it had been towed home after a mishap elsewhere in the pines." (McPhee 1967, 10-11).

Photo courtesy of Doug Brown

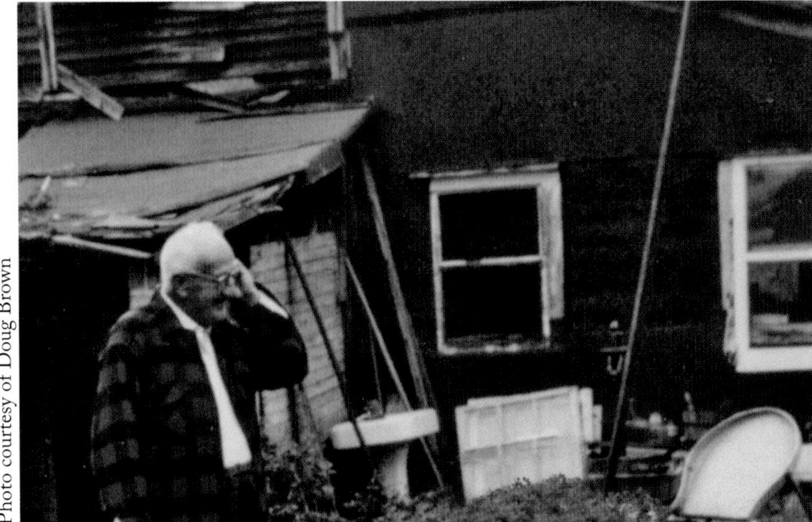

Fred Brown at his home in Hog Wallow in 1969

Emil reminisces about playing the guitar at the Albert Hall.

Blueberry and Cranberry Farmer

Sammy Moore III

"We're all family out here."

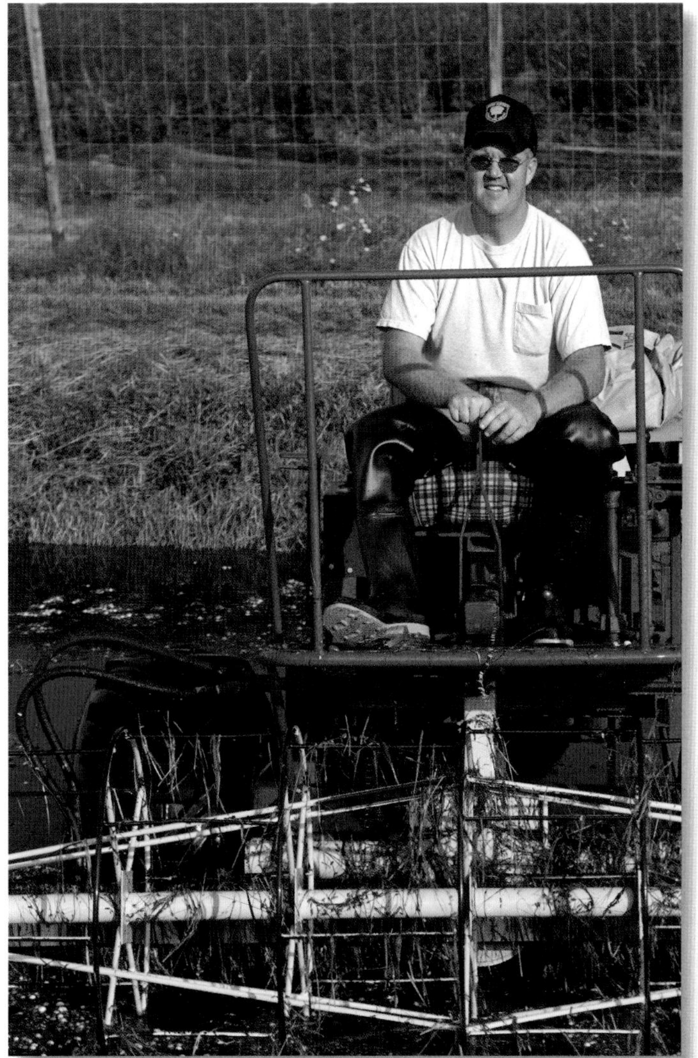

Moore's Meadows Road winds through an oasis of blueberry and cranberry farms near Wharton State Forest. At the northern end of the road is the farm of Sam Moore Jr. and his son Sammy Moore III. The farm's origin goes back to the late 1880s when Aaron Bishop Moore owned more than 1,000 acres of Moore's Meadows. Aaron had eight children and divided the farm up for his children. Over the years, Sam Moore Jr. has purchased parcels of the land from family members to acquire 650 acres of Moore's Meadows.

"We're all family out here," proclaims Sammy. "We look out for each other." When the dams blew out in 2004 due to heavy rain and threatened to flood Sammy's fields, neighboring farmers Bill Haines and Stephen Lee sent over water pumps and lent a helping hand. "Many people have their own conceptions about the Pineys, but look at my dad and the other farmers around here—they're the smartest people I know."

Sammy feels that the farmers in the Pines are good stewards of the land and necessary for the survival of the forest. The number of acres under cultivation is typically a small part of the total acreage owned by a farmer. The rest, known as headlands, are necessary to ensure a supply of good clean water, which ultimately benefits the entire ecosystem.

Early in 2007, Sammy and his family, now living in nearby Chatsworth, will move back to the farm into a new home he and his dad built overlooking the fields and bogs where they both were raised. Sammy's greatest wish is that one or both of his young sons, Sammy Moore IV and Mathew, will go on to become the seventh generation of Moore farmers.

Above: The sign at Moore's Meadows Farm

Opposite: Sunrise on Moore's Meadows Farm

Sammy III sorting blueberries

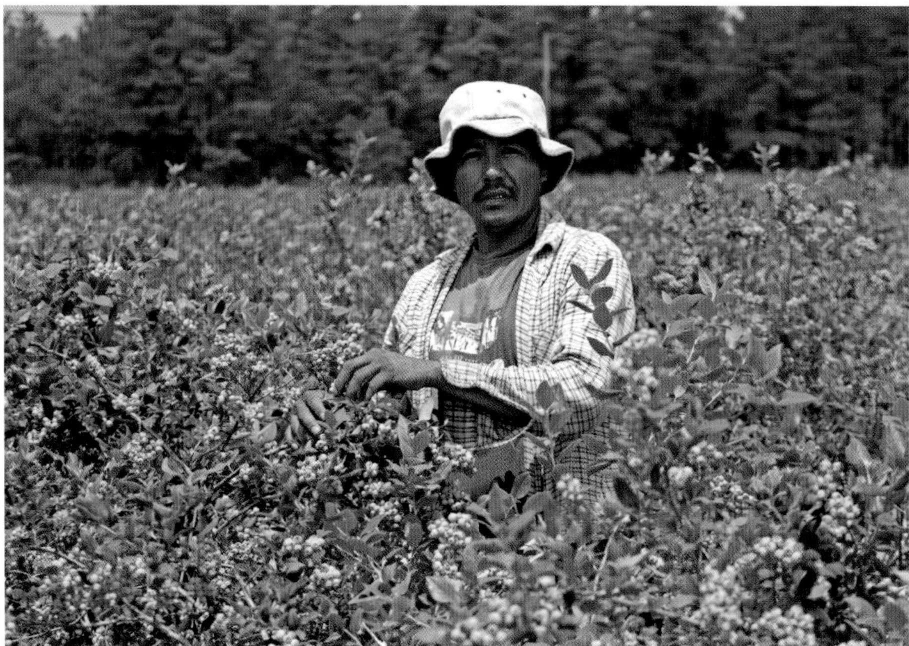

Workers harvesting the blueberry crop

Sam Moore Jr. and his grandsons, Sam Moore IV (left) and Mathew (right)

Sammy III harvesting cranberries

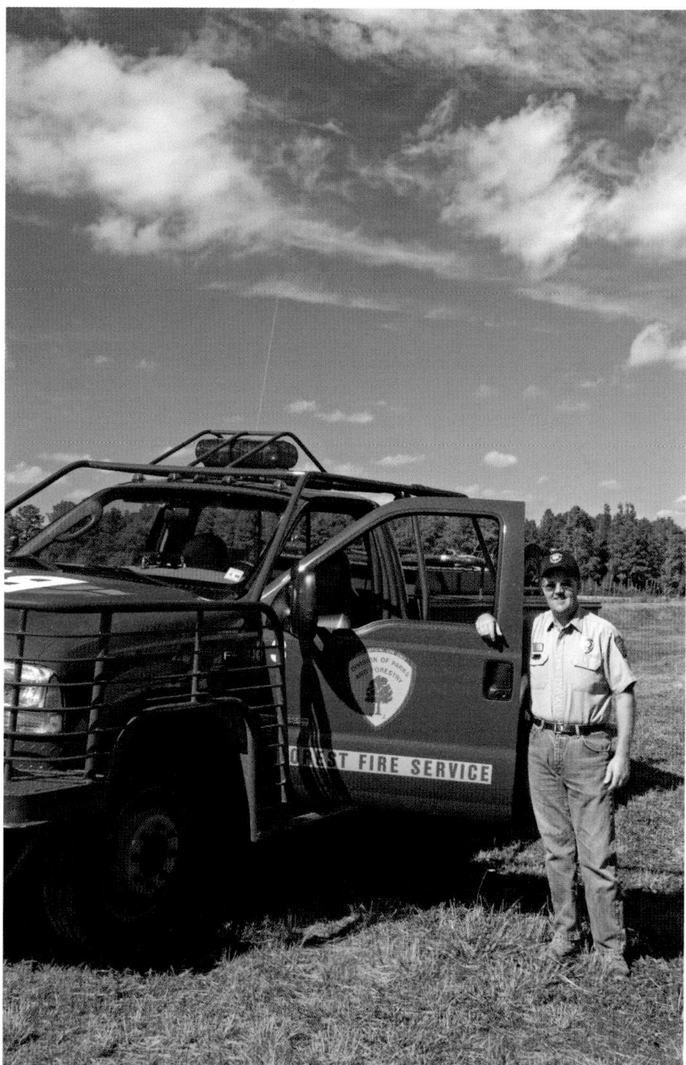

Sammy III is the local Forest Fire Warden and is responsible for an area covering 86,000 acres.

Scenes from Moore's Meadow

Opposite: Dawn at Moore's Meadow

Ecologist and Researcher

Walter F. Bien, PhD

"I've always had one foot in the pine forest and one foot in the salt marsh."

Walter F. Bien, PhD, is Drexel University's Director of Pinelands Research. "But," he says, "I've always had one foot in the pine forest and one foot in the salt marsh."

That explains his two major current projects. The first is a series of ecological studies at the Warren Grove Gunnery Range, located in the Pine Barren's unique Pygmy Forest. Although regularly disturbed by military ordinance, the range is valuable as part of the largest uninterrupted stretch of forest left in the Pines. Walt's studies include an inventory of plant and wildlife and effects of fire on the Pygmy Forest. These studies for the military have led to discoveries of how threatened pine snakes utilize bomb craters for dens and how best to restore abandoned gravel pits to their original state.

The second project is a study of the population and habitat of the Northern diamondback terrapin on the Barnegat bayshore. Walt co-leads the effort to trap, tag, track, and take blood samples and census the population of diamondback terrapins at the 180-acre Lighthouse Center in Waretown.

As a young boy growing up in Philadelphia, Walt spent his summers in Browns Mills, NJ. The family's cabin was part of a summer resort surrounding Mirror Lake, with its "life enhancing tea-colored waters" and fresh pine-scented air. It was young Walt's job to transport five gallons of water daily from the local well to the cabin, which sported a privy, but no electricity or running water. Baths were taken in the nearby lake and food was cooked on a kerosene stove.

After 31 years in public education, Walt returned to his childhood haunts with a PhD that focused on sphagnum moss ecology. He now teaches ecology courses, leads Drexel students on field trips to the Pines and bayshore, and involves them in his research projects.

Above: Diamondback terrapins

Opposite: The Pygmy Forest

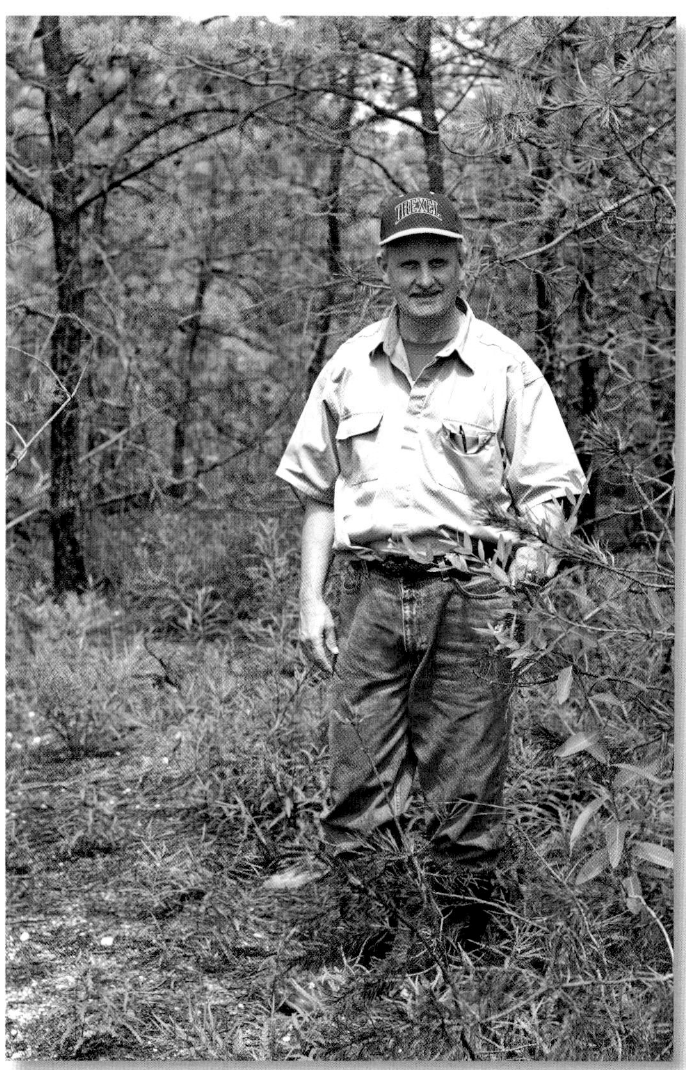

Diamondback terrapin

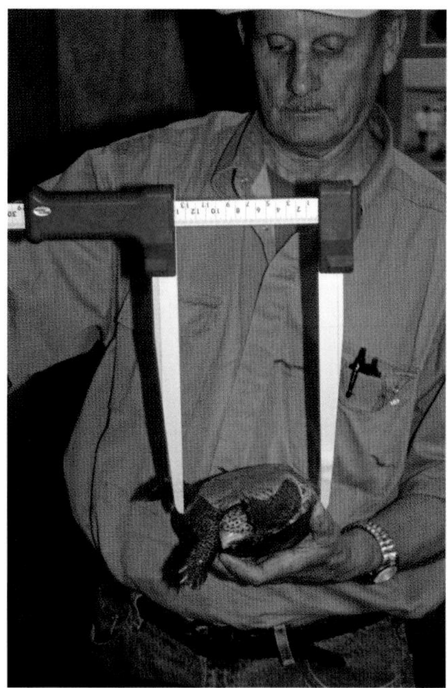

Walt measures a captured diamondback.

Walt sets the traps.

Walt and student Ron Smith use telemetry to locate a pine snake.

Pine snake

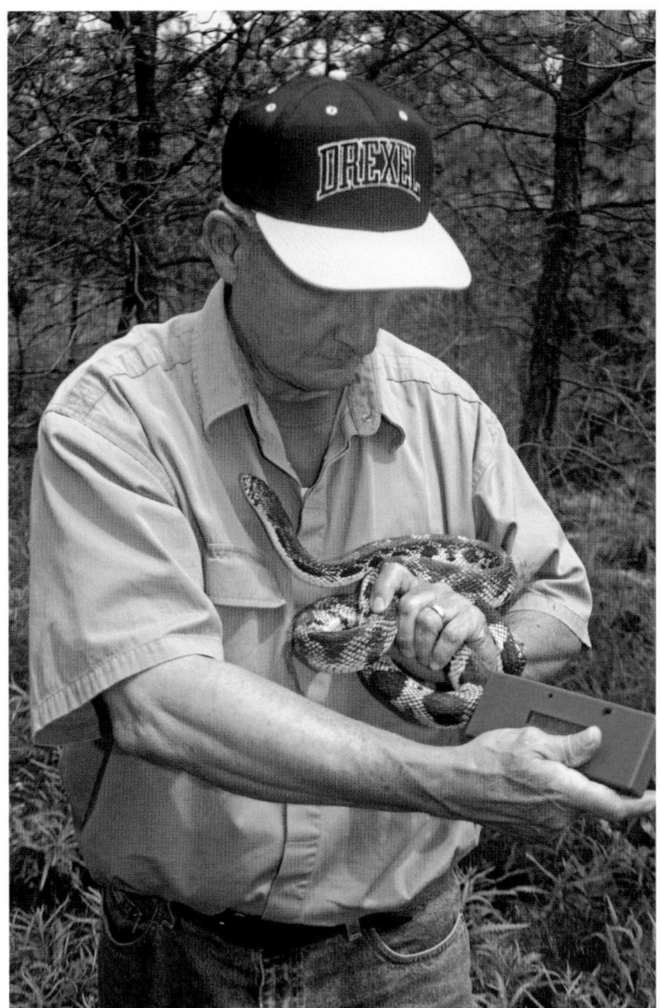

Walt takes a blood sample from a captured pine snake.

At the Warren Grove Gunnery Range, Walt stands in a gravel pit, an example of an area before restoration.

Walt inspects a recovered area five years after having been planted with native plants.

The Pine Barrens tree frog is one of the endangered species that resides in the gunnery range.

Pine Barrens rattler

Sphagnum Moss

Sphagnum moss, also called "peat moss," carpets the floor of Pine Barrens cedar bogs where it plays an important role in the local ecology. Subtle differences in the 25 species of sphagnum found in the Pines allow some species to live underwater, in wet depressions, or on higher drier ground called hummocks. Acting like a sponge, some species soak up enough water to hold 15 times their dry weight, remaining moist even after surrounding wetlands have dried out. During summer droughts a variety of animal life utilizes sphagnous bogs as refuge and a water resource.

Several plant species grow in or are associated with sphagnum, including Atlantic white cedar, orchids, and bog asphodel, while microorganisms living among its tiny leaves serve as a food source for dragonflies, mosquitoes, and frogs. Certain bacteria found in sphagnum play an important role in the nitrogen cycle, while other bacteria oxidize iron—an important step in the formation of bog iron.

Historically, piney woodsmen and "mossers" collected and sold sphagnum for use in the floral trade, as well as for making diapers and bandages. During World War I, sphagnum's acidic and antibacterial properties made it a popular field dressing for wounds. Today many of sphagnum's traditional uses are served by manmade products, and only a few "mossers" remain to eke out any economic rewards from this once thriving local industry.

Text by Walt Bien, PhD

Wildlife Biologist and Outdoorsman

Pete McLain

"When he sees something that could be made better, he makes it happen." —Diane Bennett-Chase, naturalist at Island Beach State Park

Paul "Pete" McLain, a professional wildlife biologist, is the quintessential outdoorsman and a visionary when it comes to conservation and natural resources. In his 36 years at the New Jersey Division of Fish and Wildlifc, hc cstablished the first non-game endangered species program in the U.S., which became a model for the nation. He negotiated international agreements to protect migratory shorebirds, brought ospreys, peregrine falcons, and bald eagles back from the brink of extinction, and began the reestablishment of flourishing bald eagle and peregrine falcon populations in New Jersey.

Pete was often found in his waders, helping to erect 50 pole platforms at Island Beach State Park, placing chicks in the nests, and banding fledglings. There were only 50 active osprey nests in the state when the program began in 1973; by 2006 there were more than 370 state wide, fledgling over 700 ospreys.

Bald eagles have been another passion for Pete, who helped pioneer the method of transferring bald eagle chicks from Manitoba, Canada, to nesting towers on the Delaware Bay and fledging the chicks successfully so they would return to breed in New Jersey. When the project began, there was one infertile bald eagle nest in New Jersey; by 2006 there were approximately 75 productive nests in the state.

Even while initiating and implementing these programs, Pete somehow found time to acquire over four thousand acres of wildlife habitat for the state.

An avid hunter, photographer, and writer, Pete wrote an outdoor column for the *Asbury Park Press* for 45 years and was a regular contributor to several sportsmen's magazines as well as to *National Geographic.* He has received many honors over the years, including the National Oceanic & Atmospheric Administration (NOAA) Environmental Hero Award in 2005.

Above: Bald eagle

Opposite: An osprey pair at the nest

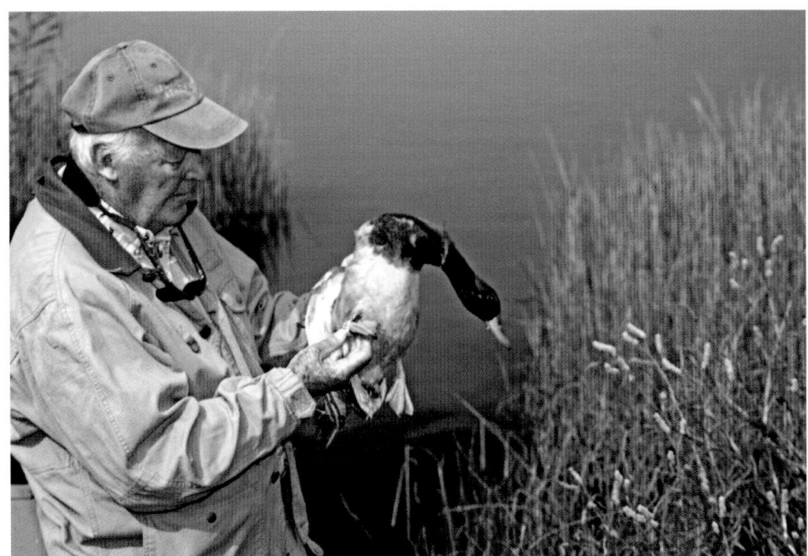

Pete bands a drake mallard.

Pete with a 1929 Model A Ford Beach Buggy at the Forked River Interpretive Center at Island Beach State Park

Opposite: Pete's dog Monty retrieves the last black duck of the day.

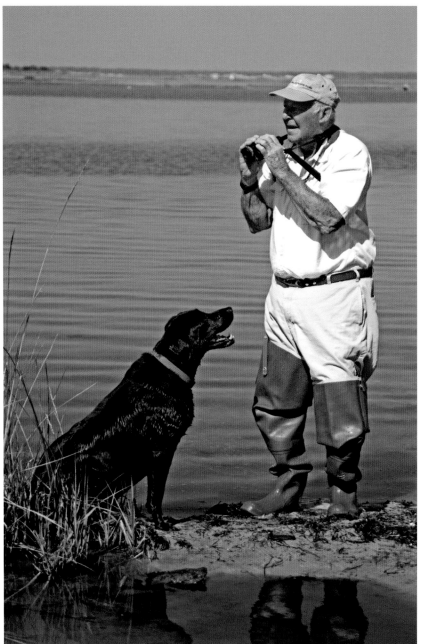

Pete and his labrador retriever Monty

LEE ANN B

Bayman

Bob Wilson

"Less clammers all the time, it's just harder to make a living now."

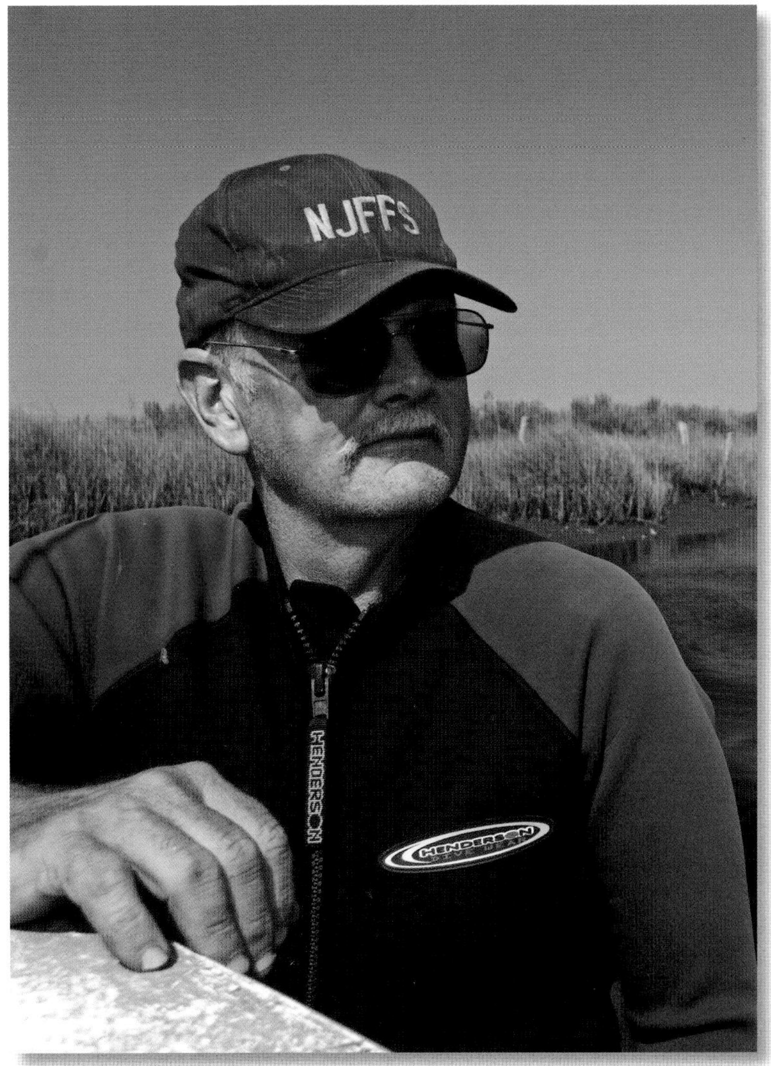

Bob Wilson motors out to Great Bay each day in his 21-foot Carolina skiff and climbs overboard to check his clam beds. A fourth-generation clammer whose grandfather raked clams for more than 50 years, Bob began to follow the family trade at age seven. He's been at it full time for 36 years and can harvest a thousand clams on a good day.

Bob's family has operated Wilson's Clam Shack on Oyster Creek in Leeds Point for 86 years, but he says it's become increasingly difficult to make a living as the supply of natural clams continues to deplete.

Not content to let his livelihood fade away, Bob and four other clammers have built their own hatchery in Brigantine to produce seed clams. He planted 70,000 seed clams three years ago and has now begun to move them to other spots where they will have room to grow.

At one time Bob acted as a guide for duck hunters, but gave it up to concentrate on clamming. He lives in Port Republic with his wife Sharon and their son and daughter, and finds time to be active in the community. He serves as a captain with the volunteer fire department and as deputy district warden for the New Jersey Forest Fire Service. "I haven't missed a major fire in the Pine Barrens for 10 years," he says proudly.

Bob Wilson's roots go deep and he loves the bayman's life, despite going out on the bay in 7°F winter weather when he has to break ice to get to his beds. There are fewer clammers every year, he says, and competition from out of state is driving prices down while costs continue to rise. It's a tough life, but he loves the hard work, tradition, and freedom that come with it.

Above: Wilson's Clam House sign

Opposite: Oyster Creek at dawn

Bob harvests his clams as the *Black Whale*, a boat on its way to Atlantic City, cruises by in the background. He wears his "rice paddy" hat to shield his face from the sun.

From raking the clambeds to packaging the clams for the market, it's a long but satisfying day for Bob.

Opposite: Bob heads back to shore in his Carolina skiff.

4WD
4WD

Foxhunter

James "Snuffy" Fisher

"Damn coyotes are ruining everything."

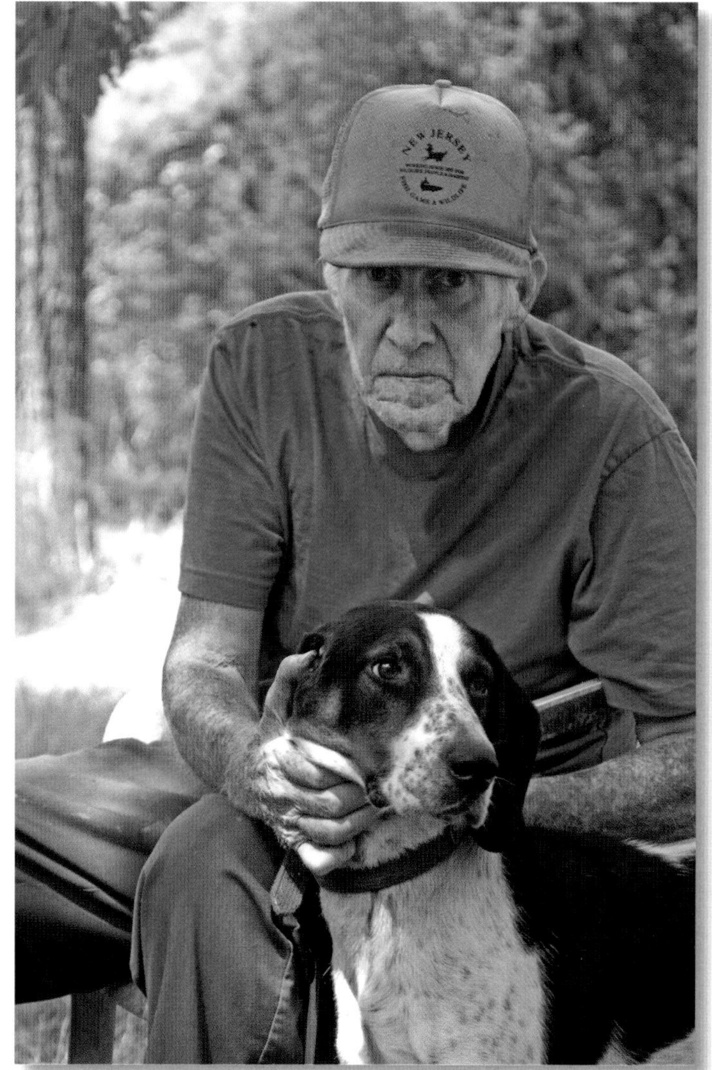

As he has on most mornings for the past 45 years, James "Snuffy" Fisher walks from his cabin deep in the heart of the Brendan T. Byrne State Forest and gathers his Maryland hounds for a foxhunt. The Maryland hound, although not recognized as an official breed by the American Kennel Club, is the hound of choice for most Pine Barrens fox hunters. Snuffy is one of the last of the old timers still practicing this sport, which is a longtime Pine Barrens tradition. Fox "chasing" might be a better way to describe the activity: The foxes are always allowed to escape, perhaps to be pursued another day.

While slowly driving the sand roads in his pickup truck, Snuffy is followed by 15 of his hounds eagerly "trailing" to pick up the early-morning scent of a fox. Once the strike dog picks up the scent, it's off to the races and the woods are filled with the sound of baying hounds in pursuit of the fox. This sound of the dogs is music to the ears of foxhunters. Using their knowledge of the woods and behavior patterns of foxes, the hunters are able to position themselves where the fox will cross the road with the hounds in hot pursuit. If the hunters feel the fox is getting too tired, or if the dogs get too close to the fox, they will break off the hunt and recall the dogs.

Snuffy, spitting some tobacco juice, laments for the future of the sport. "Most of the old-timers have passed on and the youngsters are just not picking it up," he says. He also believes that the proliferation of coyotes in the Pine Barrens is having a serious impact on the fox population. Snuffy's cousin Harry Irons frequently visits him in the woods and joins in on the hunts. Harry has coonhounds that he runs at night, but lately he keeps loosing his glass eye in the woods, which, Harry allows, makes night hunting mighty difficult.

Above: The sign on Snuffy's cabin

Opposite: The early morning start of the hunt

Snuffy and his cousin Harry Irons get ready for a hunt.

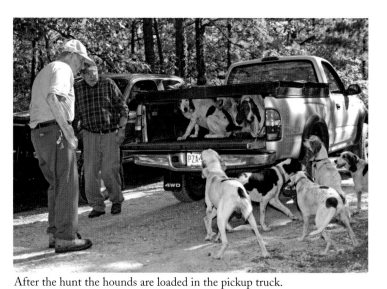

After the hunt the hounds are loaded in the pickup truck.

Snuffy's cabin in the Pines

Hounds on the hunt and (inset) a fox rests and yawns.

Pomeroy Crossroads

Deep in the heart of Brendan Byrne State Forest is a monument dedicated to the legendary foxhunter Donald Pomeroy. Pomeroy was killed in 1985 when his pickup truck went out of control and crashed into a pine tree the day before deer season opened. The following description of Pomeroy's funeral service is taken from Mary Hufford's fine book, *Chaseworld: Foxhunting and Storytelling in New Jersey's Pine Barrens* (Philadelphia: University of Pennsylvania Press, 1992: pp 36-37):

> Pomeroy's funeral service was held in Lebanon State Forest during deer week. According to those who attended, a funeral caravan of thirty-two vehicles processed slowly along the Blacktop Road toward Pasadena. First came the funeral limousine, followed by Pomeroy's wife, Patsy, and their son, Donald … and Jeff Powell drove the pickup truck that came next, carrying Pomeroy's foxhounds … Deerhunters for whom Pomeroy had served as a guide emerged from their gun clubs and stood in a row. One man on each end held a gun, "No guns in the middle," Norman emphasized.
>
> "They all lined up along the road," he said, "and they was just at attention when we went by. Beautiful."
>
> "And when the hearse went by," added Caroline, "they all took their hats off and crossed their hearts with 'em and stood at attention, till the procession got by" (interview, January 24, 1986).

The hounds are said to have watched in silence as the minister read the Twenty-Third Psalm and delivered the eulogy.

After the funeral Patsy distributed Pomeroy's hounds among his foxhunting buddies: four to Yellow Bird, four to Dogman, three to Piggy.

Above: Monument at Pomeroy Crossroads with hound and fox carving

Cranberry Farmer and Inventor

Tom Darlington

"It was thought the land was useless, but
Grandfather Fenwick knew better."

Tom Darlington's roots go back to the early days of New Jersey's cranberry and blueberry industries. In the late 1850s his great-grandfather James Fenwick purchased 300 acres of land from his cousin Benjamin Jones. "It was thought the land was useless, but Grandfather Fenwick knew better," Darlington said. The land ultimately became Whitesbog and was the first farm to intentionally create and plant a cranberry bog where there hadn't been a bog before. By the early 1900s Whitesbog was the largest cranberry farm in New Jersey. Tom's aunt, Elizabeth White, brought Dr. Frederick V. Coville to Whitesbog and developed the cultivated blueberry with the help of local Pineys.

Despite this family tradition, Tom wanted nothing to do with berry farming. "I was very happy designing aviation gas turbine parts for Westinghouse," he says. However, in 1948 Tom's brother Joe died in a plane crash at the Whitesbog airstrip. In 1950 the family asked Tom to return and run the farm. Tom agreed, with the understanding that he would also design machinery for the cranberry and blueberry industries.

The dry-harvest cranberry picker (right) was Tom's most important invention. It decreased labor from 150 scoopers to a crew of 15 machines. Tom also invented the blueberry-picking machine, a vehicle that straddles the rows of bushes and shakes the berries into receiving plates below.

In 1966 the state purchased Whitesbog. The family retained 500 acres at Buffin's Meadows, where Tom and his sons Joe and Mark built bogs using new designs. Due to improvements in technology and bog design, the yield of the Darlington's 150 acres of new bogs exceeds that of his grandfather's 600 acres.

Tom Darlington served as president and CEO of J. J. White Inc. for 45 years and was on the board of Ocean Spray for 35 years. He was one of the original members of the Pinelands Commission and according to Carleton Montgomery, Executive Director of Pinelands Preservation Alliance, "was one of the most courageous proponents of Pinelands preservation."

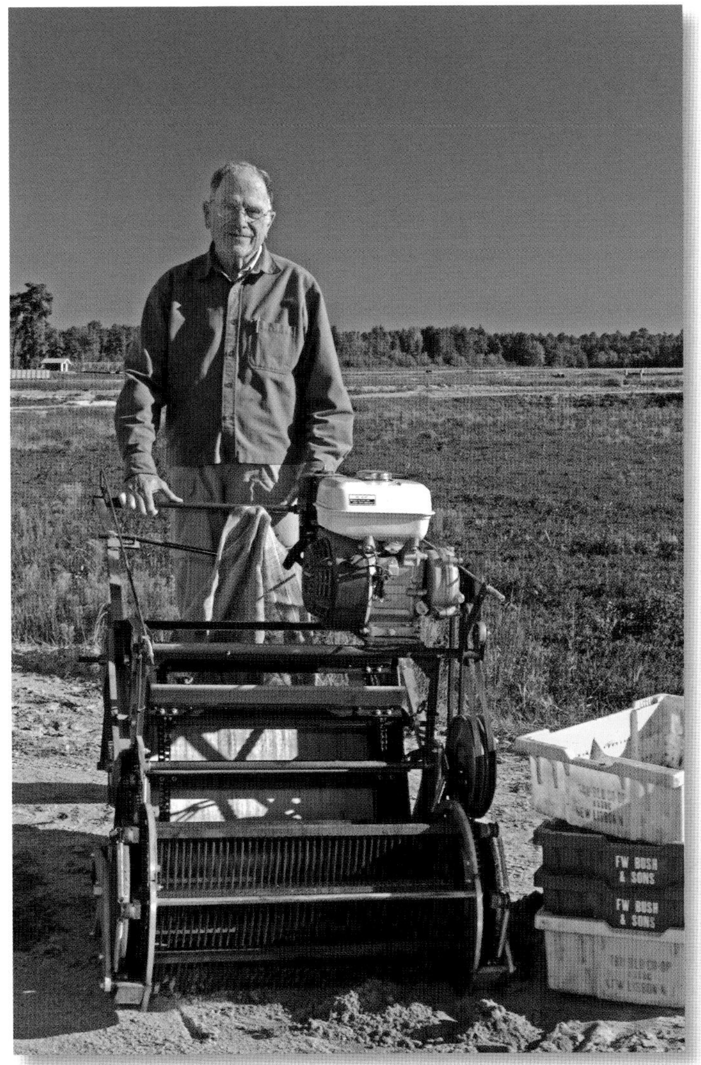

Opposite: Mike Green heads out to the bogs at dawn on a riding harvester.

Joe Darlington and Brenda Conner

Joseph "Joe" Darlington is the fifth generation of his family to own and operate the J. J. White Cranberry Company at Whitesbog. Brenda Conner traces her ancestry back to the Lenape Indians of South Jersey and is the fifth generation of cranberry farmers in the Cutts family, also cranberry and blueberry growers.

"Innovation" is the watchword as Brenda and Joe strive to improve their operations and protect their Piney heritage. They farm their cranberry bogs using Ocean Spray's Integrated Pest Management (IPM) practices and GPS technology, significantly increasing their yield. The harvester operator is guided by a laptop on the dashboard rather than by rows marked by poles, increasing accuracy from within feet to within inches.

Brenda is both an historian and folklorist. She is proud of the skills she has learned from old-time residents who work the Piney cycle, from basket making to trapping. She incorporates this lore and know-how into the bus tours she conducts in the bogs during the harvest season. She also presents "Cranberry Connection Road Shows," giving presentations on various aspects of Pine Barrens life, including Piney Lifestyles, Cranberry and Blueberry Farming, and Pinelands Industries.

Joe and Brenda are fiercely proud of their heritage and of the role Pineys play in the culture and history of southern New Jersey. Says Brenda, "The status symbol of a Piney is how far off the blacktop you live." Joe and Brenda are concerned that encroachment and increased regulation will, over time, take a toll on the people who pursue traditional work.

"If you destroy the Piney culture, you will destroy the Pines," Brenda declares.

A Cranberry Connection bus tour during the cranberry harvest

Photo by Tom Shuff

Brenda demonstrates the traditional art of basket making.

Photo by Tom Shuff

Joe opens a floodgate at dawn.

Pages 126-127: Harvesting at dawn guided by GPS technology, from left to right: Scott Carrasquillo, Mike Green, and Rodney Robins

CAUTION

CAUTION
CAUTION

Suningive, Elizabeth White's former residence

Elizabeth White

Elizabeth Coleman White was born in 1871, the eldest daughter of Joseph Josiah White, a successful farmer, inventor, and businessman. Her mother Mary A. Fenwick White was the daughter of Whitesbog founder James Fenwick. When Elizabeth began working at the family cranberry farm at Whitesbog in 1893, at the age of 22, it is unlikely she had an inkling of the critical contributions she would eventually make to the blueberry farming industry in New Jersey and beyond.

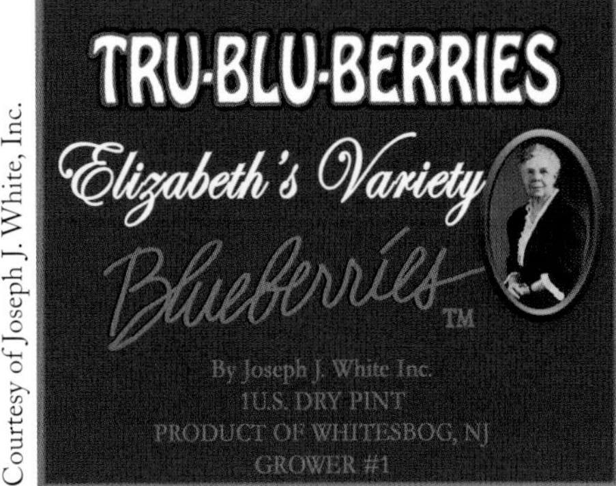

Courtesy of Joseph J. White, Inc.

From the start, Elizabeth was an active participant in the farm's management and was soon looking for a crop to complement cranberry production. In 1911 she read a paper on blueberry cultivation by Dr. Frederick V. Coville and, intrigued, invited Coville to Whitesbog to extend his experiments. Before long she was soliciting local Pineys to identify promising wild blueberry bushes. She organized her field force under two foremen, equipping the searchers with jars, labels, and aluminum gauges; bushes producing berries too large to pass through a 5/8-inch hole were brought to Whitesbog and subsequently cultivated. Frequently named after their finders, the most outstanding bush was found near Chatsworth by Ruben Leek. Dubbed the "Rubel," the fruit produced by this bush remains one of the best-known varieties of cultivated blueberry.

In 1916 Elizabeth and Dr. Coville produced their first salable crop, thus launching a new industry—blueberry farming—that would soon spread to many other states.

Elizabeth White went on to found the Tru-Blu Cooperative with Stanley Coville, Dr. Coville's son. Joe Darlington and his wife Brenda Conner purchased the Tru-Blu brand when the co-op dissolved and plan to market a variety named the Elizabeth.

In 1923 Elizabeth built a house at Whitesbog, which she named Suningive. She lived there until her death in 1954 at age 83. Sunigive has been restored, and the Whitesbog Preservation Trust offers tours of the house and gardens.

Elizabeth made a lasting contribution to the Pine Barrens, the state, and the farming industry. Because of Elizabeth White and her passion for her work, there are nearly 7,500 acres of blueberries under cultivation in New Jersey today, and the state is the second in the U.S. in highbush blueberry production.

Opposite: Whitesbog in the Fall

ALBERT HALL

Music Lover

Naomi Stackhouse

"I'd rather dance than eat!"

Every Saturday night, just before the show starts, the crowd at Albert Music Hall in Waretown surges to its feet to sing "The Star Spangled Banner." Standing in the front row and singing lustily is Naomi Stackhouse, a spry 92 year old.

Naomi has been coming to hear the Piney music since 1962, when she first went to the "Home Place," Joe and George Albert's hunting cabin in the Forked River Mountains. Naomi was one of many who brought homemade goodies to go with the coffee and good fellowship. The Alberts started their Saturday night musical tradition in the 1950s and the shows moved to Waretown in 1974 after George passed away.

Naomi was born in Barnegat and moved to Waretown when she married in 1936. She's been there ever since. As a young woman she picked blueberries, sorted cranberries, and worked in a clam house. She passed on her love of music to at least two of her five children and is proud to say her sons Jack and Jimmy played guitar and performed with the Albert Brothers.

Many of the traditions Naomi Stackhouse remembers from the Home Place continue at Albert Hall. Homemade cakes and hot coffee are served and players still jam in the parking lot and the Pickin' Shed. She likes to reminisce about dancing at the shows in bygone years. "I'd rather dance than eat!" she exclaims with a sweet smile and a twinkle in her eye.

Above: Naomi with George Albert's daughter (left) Elaine Boshko and granddaughter Leslie Derwinis at Albert Music Hall

Opposite: The Sugar Sand Ramblers on stage at the Albert Music Hall

George Albert

All photos on this page courtesy of Pinelands Cultural Society

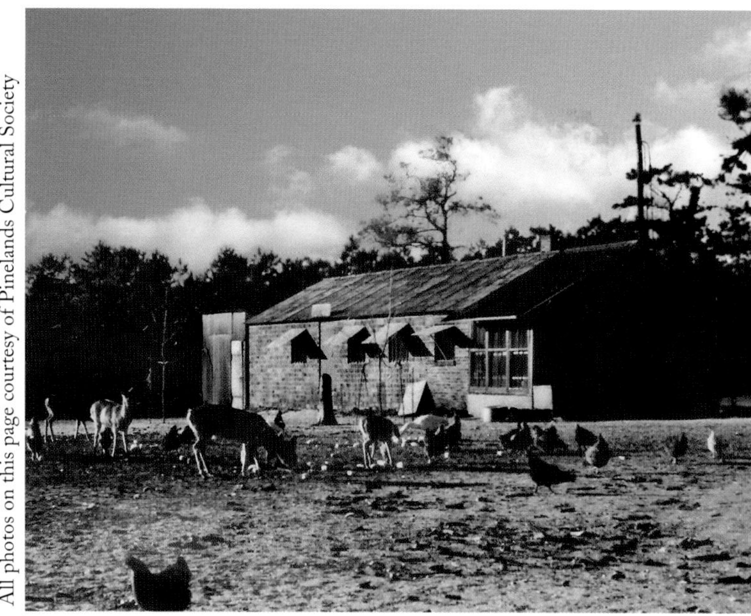
The Home Place, the Alberts' cabin where the tradition started

Joe Albert

The Albert Music Hall Story

In the early 1950s, George and Joe Albert's hunting cabin deep in the woods near the Forked River Mountains became the gathering place for a handful of musicians who would come by on Saturday night to pick and sing. The cabin was known to those musicians as the "Home Place," and on Saturday nights, with Joe on washtub bass and George playing fiddle, their music resounded through the pines long into the night.

Old-timers tell of playing at the cabin by gaslight with coffee warming on the old cast iron stove. Often musicians would gather and pick outside the cabin while waiting for their chance to get inside. So the tradition began. Word spread quickly, the crowds grew, and the Home Place became the subject of newspaper and TV reports. After George's death and when the Home Place could no longer handle the crowds, Joe sadly closed down the Saturday night gatherings.

The "pickin' Pineys," however, would not be stopped and barely six months later the music rang out once again from a room at the Waretown Auction. The building was destroyed by fire in 1992, but by that time the Pinelands Cultural Society had been created with a goal of stimulating and preserving the musical heritage of the region. So the Saturday night performances of country, bluegrass, and folk music continued, first in a parking lot and later in an elementary school, until the Albert Music Hall opened in January 1997. It's fitting that the location of the hall is just down the road from the remains of the old Home Place.

If they were alive today, George and Joe Albert would no doubt be proud to see the tradition they began continuing into a new century and to hear the "Sounds of the Jersey Pines" still echoing through the woods on Saturday nights.

Opposite: Scenes from the Pickin' Shed (Photos by Jeff Hirsch)

Pages 134–135: A gathering of musicians at Albert Music Hall (see page 146)

MUSIC
ERT HALL
UE GRASS-FOLK-OLD TIMEY MUSIC
RDAY NIGHT 8:00 P.M.
CHILDREN UNDER 12-FREE

ALBER

HALL

Naturalist and Storyteller

G. Russell Juelg

"Nonprofit organizations: entities you support in the hope they can do what the government was supposed to have already done."

Russell Juelg became intrigued with the New Jersey Pine Barrens while attending Tom Brown Jr.'s Tracker School. The former Marine decided to move to the area and took a job at Woodford Cedar Run Wildlife Refuge in Medford. He began teaching survival and wildlife courses and became managing director in 1996. In 1999 Russell began working with Pinelands Preservation Alliance (PPA) as director for outreach. He is the author of *New Jersey Pinelands: Threatened and Endangered Species* and is currently working on a second book, *The South Jersey Rare Plant Workbook.*

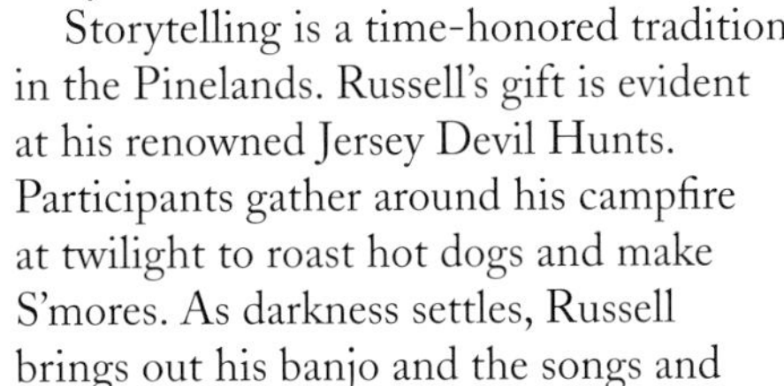

Storytelling is a time-honored tradition in the Pinelands. Russell's gift is evident at his renowned Jersey Devil Hunts. Participants gather around his campfire at twilight to roast hot dogs and make S'mores. As darkness settles, Russell brings out his banjo and the songs and stories begin. Pacing around the fire, Russell beguiles his listeners and, finally, slips into the story of the Jersey Devil. Then, with some trepidation, the group sets off through the moonlit forest on a mile-long hike in search of the Devil. Coming up short at each sound, they trail behind their spell-binding guide, and many claim to have glimpsed a ghostly form in the woods. Russell conducts between 20 and 25 Jersey Devil Hunts per year for PPA and also leads survival courses, canoe trips, and hikes along the 50-mile Batona Trail.

Endangered species are Russell's passion and he works assiduously to protect them. He initiated the Partnerships for New Jersey Plant Conservation on behalf of PPA, spurred by a lack of state regulations. Whether the subject is rare flora or Pine Barrens legends, it seems that "preservation" is Russell Juelg's middle name.

Above: A bobcat, an endangered species in the Pine Barrens

Opposite: The Jersey Devil, artwork by Patrick M. Brennan © 2007

ANY
TIME

Pinelands Preservation Pioneer

Nan Hunter-Walnut

"We made them toe the line."

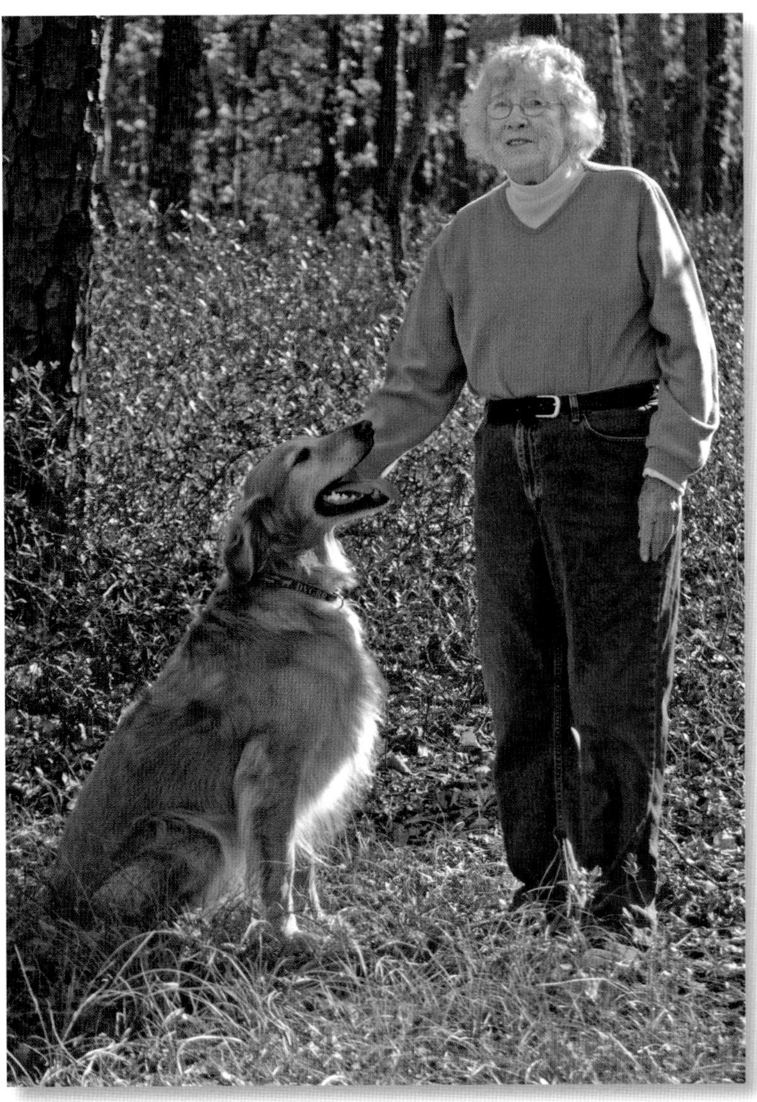

Nan Hunter-Walnut moved with her husband Rick to the Pines of Southampton Township in 1970. It wasn't long before she embraced the environment and she's been defending it ever since.

While working full time in Trenton as a legal secretary for the NJ Department of the Public Advocate, Nan and Rick found time to form the Concerned Citizens of Southampton to fight the rapid proliferation of new construction in the township. In 1977 this group became part of the Pine Barrens Coalition, and as she recalls, "we were very vocal and involved."

Pinelands Preservation Alliance

Nan was appointed to the 1977 Pinelands Review Committee by Governor Brendan Byrne. It was the committee's task to conduct economic and environmental studies and to define the boundaries of a protection area. The committee toiled for a year and a half, with farmers, sand and gravel companies, municipalities, and developers as adversaries. "We were considered a radical group," Nan recalls, "since we had no bureaucratic structure."

Bringing her activism close to home, Nan served on the Southampton planning board for 25 years. In spite of being the first environmentalist and the only woman on the board, she became its chairperson in 1995.

With the Pinelands Commission in place, the all-volunteer Pine Barrens Coalition gradually declined and was replaced by the professionally staffed Pinelands Preservation Alliance (PPA). Nan was named to the board of PPA, along with other coalition members who had fought so long for conservation. She is still active and attends Pinelands Commission hearings to speak out, echoing Brendan Byrne's concerns that protection is eroding. "I've lasted a long time," she concludes, "and I'm glad I was able to focus my efforts on the Pinelands."

Above: PPA emblem

Opposite: The barn on PPA property

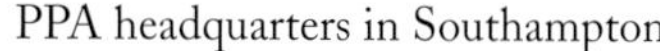

PPA headquarters in Southampton

Carleton Montgomery, Executive Director

Pinelands Preservation Alliance (PPA)

PPA was created in 1989 to act as a watchdog over the Pinelands Commission, the agency charged with implementing the Pinelands Comprehensive Management Plan, and to educate the public about the Pine Barrens. It is the only private nonprofit organization dedicated to preserving the resources of the New Jersey Pinelands.

Based in Southampton, PPA provides numerous programs throughout the year that promote the wonders of the Pine Barrens. Its "Pinelands Adventures" series includes Jersey Devil Hunts, Canoeing Piney Rivers, Ghost Town Tours, and other themed activities. Another popular program hosted by PPA is the Pinelands Summer Institute for high school and middle school science and social science teachers. This one-week program combines a mix of classroom time and fieldwork, and has provided more than 200 teachers with ideas and information to help them incorporate the Pinelands into their curricula.

The mission of PPA is "to protect and preserve the resources of the New Jersey Pinelands." The organization carries out this mission through a unique blend of staff and volunteers who travel throughout the region as advocates and educators. Through its work to educate the public and ensure strict government and industry compliance with the Pinelands Comprehensive Management Plan, Pinelands Preservation Alliance has emerged as a leading force in Pine Barrens protection and preservation.

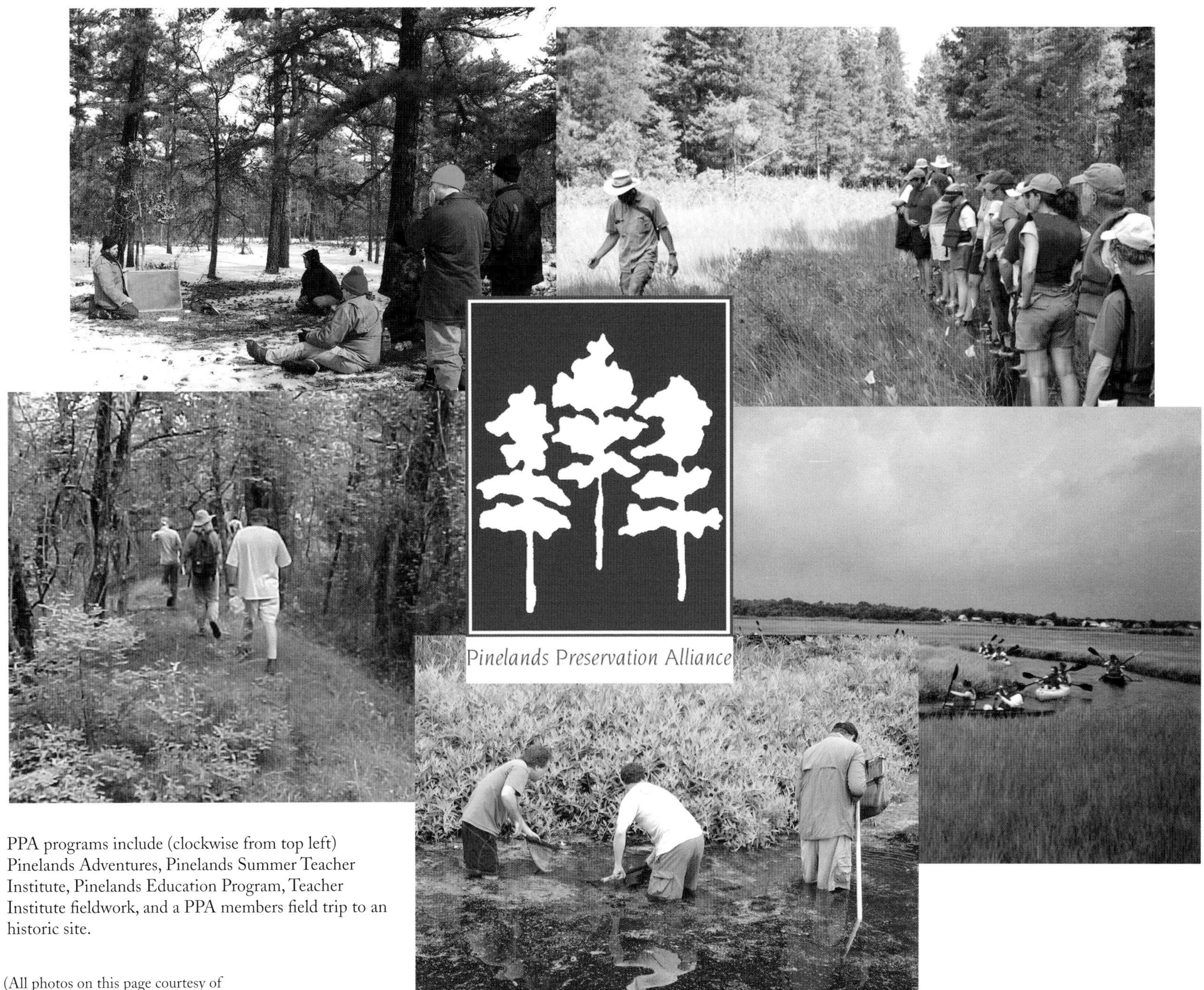

PPA programs include (clockwise from top left) Pinelands Adventures, Pinelands Summer Teacher Institute, Pinelands Education Program, Teacher Institute fieldwork, and a PPA members field trip to an historic site.

(All photos on this page courtesy of Pinelands Preservation Alliance)

Photo by Gordon Stull

Former Governors Brendan Byrne and James Florio at the 2005 Pine Barrens Hall of Fame Ceremony

In 2004, in partnership with Plexus Publishing, Inc., Pinelands Preservation Alliance (PPA) created the Pine Barrens Hall of Fame, instituting an annual award. According to Carleton Montgomery, PPA's executive director, "The award was created to honor individuals who, through dedication and hard work, have made a lasting contribution to New Jersey Pinelands preservation." Past honorees have included, among others, former New Jersey governors Brendan T. Byrne and James Florio. While a member of congress during the 1970s, Governor Florio wrote federal legislation to create a Pine Barrens Ecological Reserve. That bill ultimately evolved into Section 502 of the National Parks and Recreation Act of 1978, which formally created the Pinelands National Reserve. Early in 1979, Governor Byrne took action that led to the passage of the Pinelands Protection Act by the New Jersey Legislature on June 28, 1979.

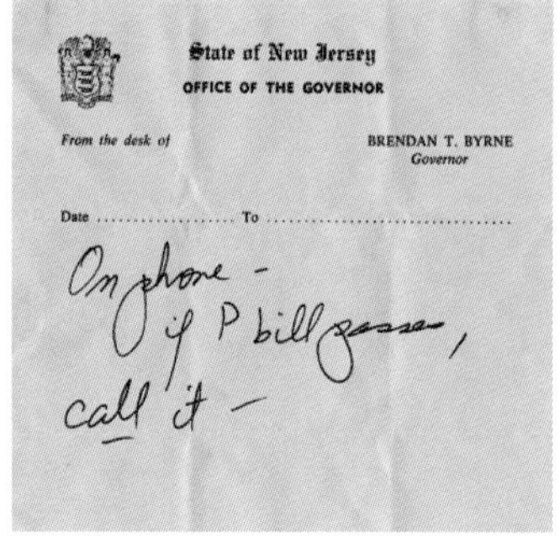

State of New Jersey
OFFICE OF THE GOVERNOR

From the desk of BRENDAN T. BYRNE, Governor

Date .... To ....

On phone -
if P bill passes,
call it -

Governor Byrne's note to call the state Pinelands bill for his signature

(Courtesy of Special Collections and University Archives, Rutgers University Libraries)

Governor

Brendan T. Byrne

"One hundred years from now, this is what I'll be remembered for."

Former New Jersey Governor Brendan T. Byrne, now in his 80s, still goes to his law office every day, plays tennis, and remains active and engaged in state affairs. A New Jersey native, Brendan is a graduate of Princeton University and Harvard Law School.

It was at Princeton where Brendan first met his close friend (and tennis partner) John McPhee, who would later go on to write *The Pine Barrens*. The Governor recalls McPhee's conclusion in the book, penned more than 40 years ago: "It would appear that the Pine Barrens are not very likely to be the subject of dramatic decrees or acts of legislation. They seem to be headed slowly towards extinction."

"I thought I could change that," Brendan says, and during his tenure as Governor from 1974 to 1982, he did, issuing a controversial moratorium on Pine Barrens development that provided time for comprehensive protective legislation to be passed. "It was a tough fight," he says, recalling the strong opposition from farmers as well as from residents worried about falling property values. The battle went to the state Supreme Court; however, the legislation, after much political jockeying, was finally passed by the state legislature one morning at 2 A.M. Prepared to act swiftly, the Governor had sent a now-historic note to his staff to immediately "call" the bill for his signature, and on June 28, 1979, the Governor signed the Pinelands Protection Act.

Many people who once opposed the creation of the New Jersey Pinelands Commission and its Comprehensive Management Plan have come to appreciate the legislation, and there is little doubt that without it the Pine Barrens would have been destroyed by rampant development. In 2002 Lebanon State Forest was renamed Brendan T. Byrne State Forest in honor of the Governor's critical role in protecting the Pines. Although he is proud of his role in Pinelands preservation, Brendan Byrne points out the need for continued vigilance. "They're starting to nibble at the edges again," he warns.

Right: Governor Byrne holds a mid-20th century cranberry scoop engraved for him in 1991 by the sponsors of New Jersey Celebrates the Pinelands.

Down a Sugar Sand Road

Small flowers softly grow; in sand as white as snow,
pink and gold in springtime, and fiery red in fall.
This quiet land is pleading, won't you please watch out for me.
There's little left where we can live, in peaceful harmony.

As I roam down a sugar sand road, around every turn and bend,
I'm greeted by wondrous scenes for which there seems no end.
But I know down deep inside, it will not last forever.
Day by day and piece by piece it will disappear forever.

(Last verse and chorus to a song written by Jim Sweet, above with his wife Carol Ann, of the Sugar Sand Ramblers, ©2000)

Photo Errata

Untitled photographs appearing in the book:
Cover and Page 150 - Emil Brown on a sugar sand road
Page i - Jim Murphy and the Pine Barons
Page ii - Lena Haines and Jimmy Cotterall at Simons Berry Farm
Page v - Jean Birdsall and the Jersey Devil
Page vi - Gerardo Ortiz at Haines bogs; Willy "Whiskers" Shaker in the Pickin' Shed at Albert Music Hall
Page vii - Ron Brewer, deer hunter and woodsman; Old '46 Ford in Moore's Meadow
Page viii - Dan Church at Simons Berry Farm
Page 146 - (above) John Hergert at the Pickin' Shed; (right) Bob Birdsall (on ladder) and John Bryans (standing) with musicians at Albert Music Hall (photo by Jeff Hirsch)
Page 147 - Charles Taylor at Lucille's Country Cooking diner

Key to the photo spread on pages 134-135 (A gathering of musicians at the Albert Music Hall, October 28, 2006), from left to right:

Front row: Laurie Dorisio, Alice Dorisio, Bruce Bunning, Bill Green, Linda Green, Gene Jardel, Karen Jardel, Charlie Constanza, Bob McGillich, Kay Mc Ilvaine, Eleonor Rosenow, Ed Ahearn, Emilee Ahearn, Daniel J. Dugan, Roy Everett, Elaine Everett, Joan A. Hansen, Pat Palatucci, Bud Palatucci, Jenny Bryans

Second row: Joe Wills, Susan Atkinson, George W. Gross, Diane Bunning, Paul Petrone, Maria Mastronardi, Leo Collins, John Channell, Judy Collins, Bonnie Leigh, Chip Crimi, Pacy Handlovsky, Carmen Hart, Susan Humen, Ralph Smith, Steve Kempf, Mac McKeown, Ron Capik, Lonnie Lynn LaCour, Gene Rosenow, Lauren Rubin, Rick Rizzi, Bob Johnson

Third row: Rich Lacey, Bill Gilsenan, Mike Garon, Robert E. Nelson, Debbie Gelormine, Stacey Tyler, Ricardo Prado, Hannah Grubow, David Rubin, Jeff Tyler, Judy Parker, Thomas Busteed

Fourth and fifth rows: Mike Edgerton, Dutch Weisgerber, John McCarthy, Zeke Parker, Florence Parker, Larry Steward, Kathi Perry, Paul Unkent, Robert E. Nelson, John Hundzynski, Lisa Garon, Laymon Cullers, Jack Cipriano, Sparky Dyer, Randy Bailey, Matt Morris, Robert Skaling-Pai, J. W. Cox, Jim Rider, Bob Nowicki, Valerie Vaughn, Heidi Olson, Jim Vasconcellos, Jared Grubow, George Tyler, Jean Tyler, Rich Bocchino, Don White, Al Suiter, Steve Yaremko, Bill Borden, John Hergert, Normon Dupont, John Bryans, Steve Yeager

Back row: Anthony Pileggi, Eddie Bodine, William Ladis, Bob Schmidt, Ed Connor, Willy "Whiskers" Shaker, John "Ozzy" Ozell

Bibliography

I would like to express our sincere gratitude to the following authors for their fine literary works on the Pine Barrens. They have been a valuable source of reference material for this book.

Beck, H.C. *Forgotten Towns of Southern New Jersey.* New Brunswick, NJ: Rutgers University Press, 1961 (reprint).

Beck, H.C. *Jersey Genesis: The Story of the Mullica River.* New Brunswick, NJ: Rutgers University Press, 1945.

Boyd, Howard P. *A Field Guide to the Pine Barrens of New Jersey.* Medford, NJ: Plexus Publishing, Inc., 1991.

Boyd, Howard P. *A Pine Barrens Odyssey.* Medford, NJ: Plexus Publishing, Inc., 1997.

Boyd, Howard P. *Wildflowers of the Pine Barrens of New Jersey.* Medford, NJ: Plexus Publishing, Inc., 2001.

Hufford, Mary T. *Chaseworld: Foxhunting and Storytelling in New Jersey's Pine Barrens.* Philadelphia: University of Pennsylvania Press, 1992.

Juelg, G. Russell. *New Jersey Pinelands Threatened and Endangered Species.* A Pinelands Preservation Alliance Publication, 2003.

McMahon, William. *Pine Barrens Legends & Lore.* Moorestown, NJ: Middle Atlantic Press, 1980.

McPhee, John. *The Pine Barrens.* New York: The Noonday Press, Farrar, Straus and Giroux, 1968.

Moonsammy, Rita Zorn. *Pinelands Folklife.* New Brunswick, NJ: Rutgers University Press, 1987.

Pavlis, Dr. Gary Charles. *The Blueberry Bulletin Vol.XXII No.22.* Rutgers Cooperative Research and Extension, 2006.

Pearce, John E. *Heart of the Pines: Ghostly Voices of the Pine Barrens.* Hammonton, NJ: Batsto Citizens Committee, Inc., 2000.

Section Forest Firewardens of Division B. *Images of America, New Jersey Forest Fire Service.* Charleston, SC: Arcadia Publishing, 2006.

Steinbeck, John. *Travels with Charley: In Search of America.* New York: Viking Press, Inc., 1962.

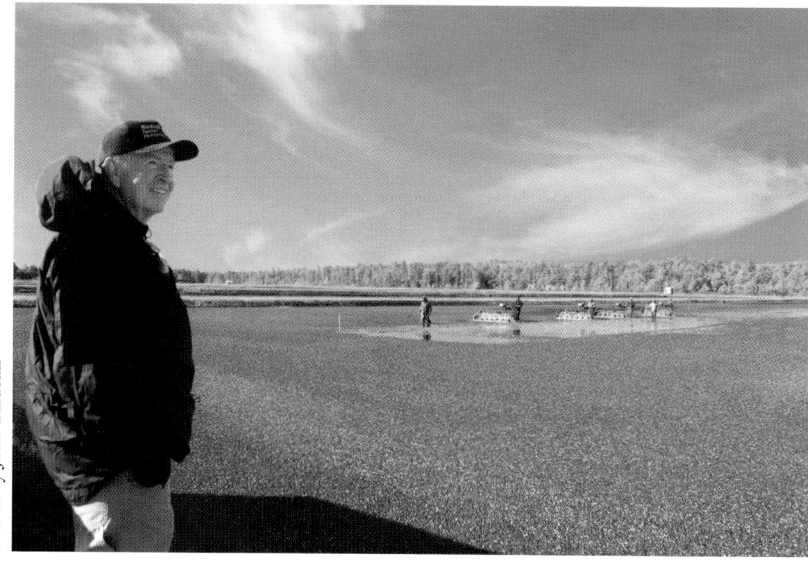

Photo by Jean Birdsall

About the Author

Bob Birdsall has been frequenting the Pine Barrens of New Jersey for more than 50 years. As a youngster growing up in Riverside, NJ, he hiked and camped in the Pines with the Scouts and, as a teenager, he hunted deer in the woods. Throughout his adult life he has returned to the Pine Barrens again and again to explore and capture the beauty of the area through his photography. His first book, *Seasons of the Pines: A Photographic Tour of the New Jersey Pine Barrens* (2004), designed by his wife Jean Sault Birdsall, presents a selection of Bob's outdoor and nature photography taken over a 30-year period.

Bob and Jean are both retired from AT&T management careers. After leaving AT&T, they spent two years in Canada where they worked as President and VP, respectively, for an international professional services company. They returned to New Jersey in 2000 to finish their professional careers with BusinessEdge Solutions, based in East Brunswick.

By combining Bob's talents as a photographer with Jean's computer and design skills ("she fixes my mistakes," says Bob), the pair is able to produce visually stunning work. *People of the Pines* is their second book about the Pine Barrens, this time focusing on the people of the region—depicted in their natural environs by Bob—and their ongoing struggles to preserve the woods and their ways of life.

Bob and Jean live in Barnegat Light, close enough to the Pines for Bob's frequent photographic expeditions that typically begin at dawn. They travel and photograph throughout the U.S. and Canada, but always return to their family, their home at the beach, and the New Jersey Pine Barrens.